P9-ARU-847

THE UNFINISHED BUSINESS

OF CIVIL SERVICE REFORM

"We cannot entrust the government of today to second-rate men and women."

THE COMMISSION ON ORGANIZATION OF THE EXECUTIVE BRANCH OF THE GOVERNMENT

THE UNFINISHED
BUSINESS
OF CIVIL SERVICE
REFORM

BY WILLIAM SEAL CARPENTER

PRINCETON, NEW JERSEY
PRINCETON UNIVERSITY PRESS
1952

Copyright, 1952, by Princeton University Press
London: Geoffrey Cumberlege, Oxford University Press
L.C. Card 52-5834

Printed in the United States of America by
Princeton University Press at Princeton, New Jersey

PREFACE

THIS book is an attempt to relate public policy to the civil service. It is neither a textbook on public personnel administration nor a statement in praise of the merit system. It assumes that appointments and promotions in the civil service on a basis of merit and fitness, to be determined in so far as practicable by competitive examinations, are wholly desirable. But the merit system has done little or nothing to enable the chief executive to utilize the public personnel to the best advantage to accomplish the purposes of government. The reform of the civil service, begun in the United States almost seventy years ago, is presently unfinished. Its completion necessitates the reconciliation of recruitment for the public service on a basis of merit and fitness with the requirement that the chief executive shall at all times be able to control the amount and quality of the administration for which he is by law responsible.

Most of the materials from which the book is constructed are identified in the text. The chief source is an extended experience in the administration of the civil service system in New Jersey. No amount of printed materials can take the place of operating experience in the formulation of public policy. There is a brief concluding chapter in which a few recommendations are set forth.

Many people have helped me in the preparation of this book. Professors George A. Graham, David A. McCabe, Joseph E. McLean, and John F. Sly of Princeton University have read portions of the manuscript and have made valuable suggestions for its improvement. I acknowledge with thanks their friendly counsel and criticism.

WILLIAM S. CARPENTER

32717

CONTENTS

THE UNFINISHED BUSINESS

OF CIVIL SERVICE REFORM

CHAPTER I

THE NATURE OF PUBLIC EMPLOYMENT

PUBLIC employment in recent years has been attracting in increasing numbers the graduates of schools, colleges, and universities throughout the United States. This has not always been true. College and university teachers have generally been unwilling to recommend the public service to their better students. The result has been that government has not had its share of the intelligent and capable young men and women of the country. Even at the present time there are too few people who enter the public service with the intention of remaining throughout a lifetime and advancing to positions of responsibility. In other words, public employment encounters difficulty in competing with business and the professions when it seeks to attract men and women in search of a career.

The idea of a career in public employment has not always been possible of achievement in this country. In the formative period of American political institutions the business of government was regarded as very simple and no special qualifications were thought to be necessary for most public employment. A few administrators, chosen mainly for their availability to party organizations, and a force of untrained clerks, were entrusted with the public services. One supporter of Thomas Jefferson told him that the public services were "no more difficult of execution than the revolutions of a horse in a mill." To this dim view of public office, President Jackson in his Annual Message of December 1829 added that "the duties of all public offices are, or at least admit of being made, so plain and simple that men of intelligence may readily qualify themselves for their performance; and I cannot but believe that more is lost by the long continuance of men in office than is generally to be gained by their long experience." Since President Jackson was convinced that training and experience are unnecessary for public employment, it is not surprising that the belief became widespread that anybody could hold a government job and that roosting on the payroll was a pleasant pastime.

Little has been done to dispel the popular belief that a public post is a sinecure. Anthony Trollope, who wrote most of his novels while an employee of the British Post Office, thought that most people entered the civil service because an early income is desirable. "The *res angusta domi*—the want of a full exchequer at home," he said, "has had much to do with it." At the same time, Trollope recognized the danger inherent in patronage appointments. "And in this way," he said, "sinecures came to pass. When a man conceived that he had placed himself under an obligation in being allowed to draw a certain income quarterly, he was apt to think that that feeling of obligation was in a great measure the return which he was bound to make for that income. That was the return in lieu of so much work. Where was the favour if he was to work hard . . . ? And then the favour grew in amount, and the work lessened, till the civil servant was a sinecurist." This accurate appraisal of the deterioration of character which so often takes place in the recipients of political favors applies to jobholders in this country as well as abroad. Until it is recognized that a sinecure benefits neither him who gives nor him who receives, public employment will not emerge from the blight of political domination.

The predicament in which public employment in the United States finds itself arises from the use of jobs as rewards for services to the political party. It is one of the inescapable facts of public life that the candidate who succeeds at the polls must share with his supporters the fruits of victory. But the successful candidate when he assumes office gives a solemn oath that he will take care that the laws be faithfully executed. At the precise moment when party workers clamor for jobs as rewards for party services, the public official finds that he is directed by law to perform—faithfully, impartially, and justly— public services which his henchmen are not qualified to undertake. Their qualifications, if any, are limited to getting out the vote in the precincts. Most party workers are prepared neither by training nor experience to assist the man for whose election they have striven.

The use of patronage to reward party services is practiced at all levels of government in the United States. The late Secretary of State William Jennings Bryan, thrice the standard-bearer of the Democratic Party in presidential elections, inquired of the Receiver of Customs in San Domingo what positions he had at his disposal "with which to reward deserving Democrats." His interest in the patronage was revealed when he reminded the members of President Wilson's cabinet that he was in a different position from any of them. "Six million people have voted for me for President three times," said Mr. Bryan, "and many of them would like to serve the nation." Since the President had announced at the first cabinet meeting that he would be busy with the "graver problems of the nation" and would "not have time to see the swarms of people who want office," the task of distributing the patronage was gladly assumed by Mr. Bryan, whose principles of personnel administration were so well understood. The New York electorate in the gubernatorial campaign of 1950 was amused but not edified by the publication of the famous Hanley letter.

Two months before the election Mr. Hanley, who had served as lieutenant governor of the state, withdrew his candidacy for the gubernatorial position thereby enabling Governor Dewey to run for a third term. In the letter Mr. Hanley stated that he had been definitely assured that, if he would consent to take the nomination for United States Senator, he would be able to clean up his financial obligations within ninety days. He also stated that he had an iron-clad, unbreakable agreement whereby he would be given a job with the state at sufficient compensation to make his net income greater than it was at that time. The pay-off came after the election when Mr. Hanley was appointed consultant to the State Division of Veterans Affairs at an annual retainer of $16,000. This was a contract job which permitted him to continue his private law practice. Neither the Hanley letter nor the patronage deals of Mr. Bryan would bring the blush of shame to the cheeks of many public officials in this country. There might be regret that such matters had reached the press, but nowhere in officialdom or in the public mind would condemnation follow disclosure.

The characteristics of patronage transactions are much the same at Washington and among the states. The evils in the spoils system are fully recognized and sometimes avoided. A few politicians have distinguished carefully between those positions which belong in a career service and those which are available as part of the patronage. Frank Hague, the former mayor of Jersey City and for many years the titular head of the Democratic Party in New Jersey, built his organization in jurisdictions fully covered by the merit system under a state civil service law. During the period of his leadership, the Democratic Party took the offices to which they were by law entitled and paid no attention to the other aspects of public employment. If changes in the civil service system were desired, Mr. Hague was careful to see that these were made with benefit of the legislature. That is to say, the civil service law was amended to accomplish the ends sought by the Democratic Party, and the merit system was not subjected to irregular interference in behalf of party aims. In this way a strong civil service system was developed at the same time that the political party retained control of the offices at the policy-making level.

It did not escape Mr. James A. Farley, who had much to do with distribution of the patronage in the administration of President Franklin D. Roosevelt, that jobs can be harmful to a political party. "When political organizations begin thinking about jobs and nothing else," he said, "they have commenced their own death chant without realizing it." Although Mr. Farley favored the patronage system, he once remarked that with time, patience, and hard work he could construct a major political party in the United States without holding out a single job to deserving partisans. Since party organizations so often become mired in patronage squabbles, it might be expected that enlightened political leaders would strive to reduce the area within which conflicts could arise. In other words, politicians could become advocates of the merit system for wholly selfish reasons.

Political appointments are wholly consistent with an efficient public service when these are restricted to positions which involve the determination of policy. There may be occasions when such positions can best be filled by appointments from the permanent civil service, but these are not likely to be frequent. The truth is that men and women who seek a career in public employment are seldom qualified to assume the role of makers of policy. Moreover, their professional interests are ordinarily so confining that they are unable to find the time for the consideration of programs of public policy. A wise civil servant has said: "Reasonable permanency of tenure, which is at least a major part of the essence of the career service, does much the same thing to everyone regardless of whether he is a messenger or whether he holds a Ph.D. degree. . . . The demands of the service force us to concentrate on a particular line. . . . It takes the political heads to preserve perspective; the career men cannot do it for themselves; the world is too big and their own job too narrow." The evils of the spoils system lie not in the political appointments of department heads and their deputies but in its extension to the rank and file of public employees who are not primarily responsible for the formulation of public policy.

If a career is to be carved out for anybody in public employment, the foundations must be laid in the public service as it exists today. It is wholly unrealistic to point to the civil service in Great Britain or elsewhere and conclude that we should have the same system in the United States. Exotic institutions are not easily reconciled with the political heritage of the American people. The jobs that presently exist, or are about to be created, in federal, state, and local governments are the materials with which intelligent men and women must fashion their careers. The presence of an increasing number of educated and intelligent public employees will in itself constitute a powerful force for the improvement of the public service. Before a civil service growing in intelligence and in skill the obstacles to a career in public employment shrink perceptibly.

Probably no expedient is better designed to ensure competence among public employees than competitive tests for appointment. Open competition not only leads to the exclusion of the unqualified but also gives to those who succeed a sense of accomplishment. Anthony Trollope said to an audience of civil servants as long ago as 1861: "A lad who knows that he has been adjudged fit for the work which he has to do, and who bears with him into the service this mark of approbation, is taught to conceive that from the first he makes a fair bargain with the public which is his paymaster. Such a fair bargain he does make. Let him therefore eschew all idea of an obligation imposed." It is true that some people who pass civil service tests fail to adjust to the actual requirements of a public post. Neither character nor personality tests are wholly reliable. But there can be no doubt that a man who has placed himself on a civil service register has thereby gained a measure of confidence in his own worth that otherwise might be lacking.

The British experience with the merit system is highly enlightening. The creation of a career service in England became possible only when a common system of recruitment for all departments was introduced. It was found that a system of appointment wholly dependent upon patronage and conducted separately by each department led to the employment of the unambitious and indolent. The introduction of competitive examinations changed the civil service, and the fact that the public employees all entered the service through the same gate of competitive examinations did much to create a bond of unity among them. They regarded themselves from the moment they were appointed from eligible registers as belonging to a career service.

Undoubtedly too much emphasis has been placed in this country upon the security of tenure afforded under the merit system. It should not be forgotten that political expediency plays an important role in determining what jobs shall exist in public employment. The former president of the United States Civil Service Commission has

9

recently stated: "The great majority of federal civil service employees obtain their jobs by competition, on their own merit, and they retain their jobs and advance in the federal service on the same sound basis." While this is doubtless true, the very existence of jobs depends upon the willingness of public officials to support and enlarge the services within which employment is provided. There are some public services which a government cannot refuse to perform if it is to continue in existence. Less essential services may be established as a result of pressures upon the framers of public policy. Finally, a government may embark upon services solely at the whims of individuals or as a result of the tactics of politicians. From whatever source derived, the establishment of a public service creates opportunities for public employment.

Jobs are important in proportion to the importance of the tasks to be performed. A job is "Dead Sea fruit" to a man in search of a career if it does not enable him to develop to the fullest extent the talents which he possesses. There is nothing more pathetic in the public service than the employee of real ability who finds himself in a "dead end" job. He does over and over the tasks he performed in the first year of his employment and in time falters in his performance as his interest in the work declines. When he begins to invoke his years of service as the sole reason for his further advancement, he has suffered a deterioration from which he can seldom be reclaimed.

The fault lies not merely with the legislative and executive branches of the government which plan and provide the funds with which to perform the services. Blame for the wastage of human resources must lie in much greater degree at the doors of top agency administrators who strive for numbers of employees rather than quality of service. If department heads were required to show each year at budget time greater quality performance instead of larger payrolls, there might be happier civil servants as well as more efficient government.

Public employment is distinguished from that afforded by private enterprise in a number of ways. One of these is the preferential treatment guaranteed to veterans on employment. The federal government and the governments of thirty-nine states provide what is known as veterans' preference in appointments to jobs in the public service. Among the states, eight assure veterans preferential treatment in promotions and thirty-four provide advantages to veterans on retirement that are not shared by other employees. Thus the non-veteran is placed at a disadvantage when he seeks employment at Washington and in the great majority of the states.

Veterans' preference in the United States antedates the merit system and is probably more deeply rooted in popular sentiment. At the close of the Civil War, Abraham Lincoln said: "I shall at all times be ready to recognize the paramount claims of the soldiers of the nation in the disposition of public trusts. I shall be glad also to make these suggestions to the several heads of departments." For any vacant office the ex-service man had first call.

Congress was prompt to act upon the suggestion of Lincoln. On March 3, 1865, a law was passed providing that soldiers and sailors honorably discharged "by reason of disability resulting from wounds or sickness incurred in line of duty" should "be preferred for appointments to civil offices, provided they are found to possess the business capacity necessary." In this way the preferential treatment for disabled veterans became a part of the public policy of the federal government, where it has since been retained and enlarged.

Statutory preference for veterans also antedates the merit system in most states which have adopted state civil service laws. Fourteen states had adopted preference laws for veterans prior to World War I. Unlike the federal statute, which gave preference only to veterans disabled in line of duty, the state laws included all veterans, disabled and non-disabled. In all cases the legal formula was practically the same. It required honorable discharge and the business capacity necessary to perform the duties of the office concerned. If the state did not have at the same time a civil service law, there was no way whereby a veteran could proceed to enforce compliance unless by mandamus proceedings. Where a mode of enforcement either through the civil service law or mandamus proceedings was lacking, the veterans' preference statute became a law without sanctions.

The extension of preferential treatment to non-disabled veterans was never justified by elaborate arguments. The climate of opinion at the time of World War I was such that the American people readily accepted the view that veterans' preference in public employment was an appropriate means of rewarding men and women for services in the armed forces. The federal government fell in line with the states and granted preferential treatment on appointment to all veterans. Laws were enacted on March 3, 1919, and July 11, 1919, which gave preference in the executive services at Washington and in the field services to all the veterans of all the wars of the United States. This was a preference over all other persons who might be eligible to appointment. Almost all of the states which adopted veterans' preference laws embraced non-disabled as well as disabled veterans.

The Nature of Public Employment

The federal government and most of the states add points to the earned score on civil service examinations in order to establish a preference in behalf of veterans. A few states, including Massachusetts and New Jersey, grant an absolute preference to all veterans who pass civil service tests. In these states disabled veterans go to the top of civil service lists in the order in which they pass, and are followed by other veterans in the order in which they pass. Non-veterans are placed in the order in which they pass below the veterans. This was the practice established for five years in New York as a result of a constitutional amendment. When the five-year period had elapsed, New York by statute reverted to the point system.

In a few jurisdictions the points are added to the earned score although a passing mark may not have been attained initially. In other words, the additional points may be used in such cases to reach a passing mark. It is superfluous to point out that this practice violates the fundamental principle upon which veterans' preference was rested in 1865. Veterans, as well as non-veterans, were expected to demonstrate "business capacity" for the job. It is helpful neither to the applicant nor to the public service to pass unqualified persons by adding points to an earned score which is below the passing mark.

Intelligent leaders of veterans' organizations have not asked in behalf of their membership any relaxation of the requirements for competitive examinations. They have agreed that veterans, along with other citizens, must show "business capacity" for a position. What they ask is that preferential treatment in appointment shall be granted those veterans who pass civil service tests. These same leaders have generally not pressed for veterans' preference in promotions. They have acquiesced in the view that once a veteran has secured a public appointment his advancement should depend wholly upon his performance in the position. The small number of states which extend veterans' preference to promotions is evidence of the widespread belief that veterans should advance on their own merits after they have been appointed in the public service.

Veterans' preference is an exception from the normal operation of the civil service system. It must therefore be justified upon some substantial ground. Preferential treatment for veterans in public employment cannot be justified on the ground that a man has lost valuable time in civilian pursuits as a result of years spent in military service and is therefore entitled to public assistance in regaining what he has lost. Neither can it be supported by any argument that the country owes the veteran a living just because he served in its defense. Military service is one of the obligations of citizenship and should not be avoided any more than the payment of taxes. Veterans' preference can be justified only because in this way the best citizens can be encouraged to come into public employment.

There can be no doubt that war brings into the armed forces of the United States very large numbers of our ablest young men and women. World War I enlisted more than three million men in the 21 to 31 years age group. World War II brought into the armed forces many more millions of men and women in even broader age groups. Among these were the most enterprising, imaginative, and resourceful of our citizens. Of course, there were many fine citizens who for various good reasons were unable to serve in the armed forces in either war. But in the recruitment of public personnel policies cannot be fitted to individual cases. A policy must be formulated which will encourage the largest number of best qualified citizens to become candidates for public employment. This must be the sole aim of veterans' preference legislation.

The maintenance of veterans' preference on a statutory basis permits the withdrawal of the privileges when special inducements to veterans will no longer bring the most competent people into the civil service. As time passes and the veterans grow older, positions with age limits will be closed to them. There will come a time when veterans' preference will be rewarding a steadily deteriorating group of citizens, if only because the veterans will be growing older. The sons and daughters of the veterans themselves will be discriminated against when preferential treatment of veterans is unduly prolonged. There must come a time when it is no longer desirable in the public interest to encourage aging veterans to compete in civil service examinations. That time has not yet arrived.

A sound system of veterans' preference will apply only to appointments and retirements. Veterans should meet the same requirements as non-veterans in civil service examinations. But no testing procedure is so perfect that it can arrange in precise order the relative skills of large numbers of candidates. It is entirely feasible for an examiner to distinguish between those candidates who appear to possess the qualifications necessary to perform the duties of a position and those who appear to be lacking in this respect. It is also possible for the examiner to classify roughly those who are most promising of successful performance, but there is always a large element of unreliability in all decisions which seek to place one qualified candidate ahead of another. There is much to be said for allowing the appointing authority a free choice among those candidates who pass a test, instead of restricting the selection to the three or the five who stand highest on a list. It cannot therefore be claimed that great harm has come to the merit system through veterans' preference in initial appointments to the public service.

The federal government has restricted certain positions to veterans as long as such preference eligibles shall be available, and at least until July 25, 1952. The positions for which veterans only may compete include those of guard, elevator operator, messenger, and custodian. These positions in Washington have traditionally been filled by ex-service men and popular sentiment undoubtedly supports the practice.

The retirement of veterans on pension at a somewhat lower age than non-veterans can be defended on the ground that the time spent in the armed forces was actually in the public service. Some very clumsy attempts have been made to compute the time spent in the military service as a part of the civil service record of a public employee. A much simpler and more feasible arrangement would permit the retirement of a veteran from the civil service on full pension from two to five years earlier than non-veterans. Veterans should undoubtedly contribute to their own retirement allowances. Free pensions for veterans can be defended no more than preferential treatment on promotions. When the veteran has been appointed in the civil service he should receive no further advantages not shared by other citizens until he is ready to retire.

Veterans' preference may become an academic question if universal military training should be established in the United States. In a few jurisdictions the definition of veteran has been restricted to persons in the armed forces during actual hostilities. Attempts to limit veteran status to ex-service men who have served in a "shooting war" and deny similar status to men conscripted for military training or for service in an army of occupation will be bitterly opposed. It is doubtful whether this distinction can long be maintained in legislative policy. Veterans' preference has meaning only when it embraces a restricted group. The advantage which it provides is lessened in proportion as the number of persons who possess it increases. Veterans' preference will be of value to nobody when it can be claimed by everybody.

While veterans' preference may discourage some capable and intelligent young men and women from competing for public employment, more are likely to be deterred by the low salaries paid at entrance levels. This is unfortunate, because the low entering salaries are not a true measure of the rewards to be obtained from the public service. Civil service compensation plans are constructed upon the assumption that public employees will remain and advance in the service of the government. Although initial salaries are generally lower than those paid by private enterprise, the annual increments provided by civil service compensation plans soon bring public employees to the wage levels found in business. That is to say, private enterprise pays more at the start but advances salaries less rapidly, and sometimes not at all, while civil service compensation plans assure regular increases within salary ranges until the maximum is reached. In general, the maximum of a civil service range is about as much as the top salary paid by private enterprise for similar work.

There is one striking exception to this generalization: the top echelons of administration are invariably underpaid when compared with private enterprise. Bureau chiefs and others in the highest civil service positions do not command salaries comparable to those paid in banks or in manufacturing and commercial establishments for similar administrative work. The political heads of departments and their deputies, who are not under civil service regulations, are also not compensated at the levels of private enterprise. The result has been a lack of continuity in the administrative levels of most executive agencies. In discussing this situation, Secretary of Defense Robert A. Lovett said: "I do not mean to imply that government can or should compete with private business in administrative officers' salaries. In my opinion, it should not. On the other hand, it should be more realistic in meeting changed economic conditions and not let virtue wear itself out in being its own reward." Mr. Lovett suggests the creation in each executive agency of a highly placed, and presumably highly paid, administrative assistant who would enjoy reasonable security of tenure.

Most of the complaints about inadequate salaries spring from the employees in the lower salary brackets. If these people were working for private employers, they would be organized in unions which would strive through collective bargaining to obtain for them salaries not only adequate to meet the cost of living but also fairly proportioned to wage scales paid throughout the industry. Civil service commissions, personnel boards, salary standardization boards, and similar agencies seek to obtain for public employees the same advantages. The time and energy expended in recent years by these agencies to obtain salary adjustments in public employment often exceeds that made by the unions in behalf of their members.

The results obtained by these public agencies have not always been commensurate with the efforts they have put forth. In the first place, there will always be a time lag in the processes of government because action required by a legislature or a municipal governing body can ordinarily be taken only once each year. In states where the legislature meets biennially the time lag is even greater. Budgets once buttoned up remain intact throughout the fiscal year or the biennium. During an inflationary period rapid increases in the cost of living may cause genuine hardship to public employees before relief can be afforded them unless some foresight is exercised.

It is always possible to fix salary scales so that these rise and fall according to changes in the cost-of-living index as determined by the Bureau of Labor Statistics at Washington. In order to embody an arrangement of this kind in the civil service compensation plan a reserve fund must be appropriated for possible salary increases during the period when the legislature is not in session. Fiscal planning of this kind has little appeal to the legislators or to the taxpayers. Neither group is interested in maintaining a surplus just in case this may be required for increases in the salaries of public employees. A crisis in public employment is ordinarily necessary before remedial action will be taken.

In the second place, the public employees or their spokesmen can always be counted upon to intervene when salary increases are being considered. They nearly always oppose any selective increases based upon merit and insist upon across-the-board increases for all public employees. Most public employee leaders will prefer small increases in the same amount to everybody rather than increases proportioned to merit or the importance of the position.

These across-the-board increases when proposed to the fiscal authorities are easily understood. They command respect among elective officials because they shower the greatest benefits upon the ranks of those who wield the most votes. But they distort the compensation plan and lead to great unfairness and injustice among employees. Unless increases are carefully proportioned to the worth of the services performed they are more harmful to the public service than no increases at all. There are no more bitter grievances among civil service employees than those which arise from the unfair distribution of compensation.

In the state legislatures, pay bills and tenure bills form part of the scenery at every session. These bills seek to establish higher salaries for particular classes of public employees or to give civil service tenure without examination to the incumbents of certain positions. These are bad bills, but they are often enacted into law. They are part of the small change in the graft and corruption which centers in state capitols. Sometimes bills of this kind are initiated by ad hoc groups of interested employees who collect a fund to secure the preparation and sponsorship of their measures. Special legislation of this kind is frequently encouraged by party chairmen who hope thereby to gain for the party the support of the public employees. An honest and courageous governor can readily destroy by his veto if not by conference with his legislative leaders the unsavory practice of special acts to raise salaries or grant tenure in public employment. The only pay bills or tenure bills which should be permitted to pass a legislature are those which emanate from the administration.

There are occasions when the salaries of public employees are pegged above the levels paid for comparable duties in private employment. The United States Bureau of the Census reported in 1948 that government employees in Washington were paid higher average salaries and wages than the employees of private enterprise within the same area. These occasions are rare. Of course, government has the power through taxation and borrowing to establish any compensation plan it chooses to adopt. But uneconomic public wage payments are far-reaching in their effects. When the salary scales in public employment are higher than those of private enterprise, private employers are prevented from competing with government for workers at the same time that they are forced to shoulder a heavier tax burden necessitated by the higher public payrolls. Serious political repercussions are almost certain to follow any attempt for a prolonged period to maintain compensation plans which carry higher salaries and wages for government employees than those currently paid by private employers.

Compensation plans in public employment might become a stabilizing influence in the economy of the nation. According to the figures of the Bureau of the Census issued in January 1952, the total labor force in the United States was 63,452,000 of which government employees at all levels amounted to 6,801,000. In other words, one out of every ten persons gainfully employed in this country is on a government payroll. When 10 per cent of the people who work receive their salaries and wages under a compensation plan the terms of which are or can be fixed for some time in advance, there is a reasonable expectation that the standardization of salaries in public employment will help to bring stability to salary and wage rates throughout the nation. There is no doubt that during the depression years following 1929 the army of public employees with their fixed rates of salaries and wages helped to establish a floor beneath which salary and wage rates in private industry could not be lowered.

Before compensation plans in the public service can

be highly influential in stabilizing the economy of the nation, however, they must be constructed upon the basis of accumulated facts. They must not depend upon pressure-group politics on the part of public employees. The essential facts are always available at every level of government but they are frequently ignored. The elected officials should obtain the widest range of information as a basis upon which to formulate public policy, but no government can afford to ignore its central personnel agency or its budget bureau in framing a compensation plan.

Veterans' preference and the salary scales presently being paid may deter some capable and intelligent young men and women from seeking careers in public employment. They should not have this effect. The veterans of World War II who are able to qualify as preference eligibles may be expected to decline sharply as these men and women grow older. Many public jobs do not interest veterans and there are already many vacancies for which no qualified veterans are available. Moreover, the entire question of veterans' preference is bound to be reviewed by the federal and state governments in the light of what is happening today to the youth of the country.

Compensation plans are being scrutinized with greater care than in the past to ensure their fairness. Legislatures are committed to the ideal of salaries and wages commensurate with the duties performed at the same time that they are being required to provide for appointments on a basis of merit and fitness. While salary and wage scales in public employment do not yield in all cases as large a return as those of private enterprise for similar work, wage rigidities have been overcome. In most sections of the country recruitment for public jobs proceeds uninterrupted despite the sometimes low entrance rates provided in civil service compensation plans.

A greater threat to the recruitment of the best young people for public employment looms on the horizon in the loyalty program sponsored by the federal govern-ernment and now being duplicated in part by a number of the states. The federal government and the govern-ments of at least forty-one states have long carried on their statute books laws covering subversive activities. Generally these laws dealt with sedition, and covered oral or printed utterances in which the state or the gov-ernment is held in contempt and the people are encour-aged to refuse obedience to its commands. A new and different policy was inaugurated in the Hatch Act of 1939 and reached its full flowering in Executive Order No. 9835, issued by President Truman on March 21, 1947. This policy undertakes to treat employees of the government as a special group with respect to the ques-tion of political loyalty.

The loyalty program which emerged under the aegis of the Hatch Act was designed to exclude from public employment any person who held "membership in any political party or organization which advocates the over-throw of our constitutional form of government in the United States." Under the pressure of war conditions, Congress authorized the War and Navy Departments to dismiss summarily employees considered by the de-partments to be "bad security risks." In 1946 the same authority was extended to the Department of State. The Atomic Energy Act of 1946 contained a provision that no person should be employed by the agency until the Federal Bureau of Investigation had made an investi-gation and report upon the character, associations, and loyalty of the individual. Thus in peace and war the employees of certain "sensitive agencies" were to be subjected to special conditions of employment which were not applied to other federal employees and which were not related to the prohibitions contained in the Hatch Act. The way was thereby paved in legislative policy for the executive order of President Truman, which requires a loyalty investigation of every person entering the civilian employment of any department or agency of the executive branch of the government and which holds the head of each department and agency personally responsible for eliminating disloyal employees.

Executive Order No. 9835 was declared to have a two-fold objective: first, to afford the United States maximum protection against the infiltration of disloyal persons into the ranks of its employees; and second, to afford equal protection to the loyal employees of the government against unfounded accusations of disloyalty. Subsequently, on April 28, 1951, the President issued an executive order which recites: "The standard for the refusal of employment or the removal from employment in an executive department or agency on grounds relating to loyalty shall be that, on all the evidence, there is a reasonable doubt as to the loyalty of the person involved to the Government of the United States." Although the loyalty program grants the suspected employee a hearing, it does not provide that he shall be confronted by his accusers or afford him an opportunity to cross-examine them. Indeed, he may be refused an exact statement of the charges against him if for reasons of security specific charges are deemed unwise. The process is not a judicial process.

Nevertheless, the United States Supreme Court on April 30, 1951 upheld in the case of *Bailey v. Richardson* a decision of the United States Circuit Court of Appeals for the District of Columbia (122 Fed. Rep. 2nd Series, 46). The court vindicated the procedures pursued in the loyalty program and adhered to the doctrine that, except to ensure compliance with statutory requirements, the courts will not review the action of federal executive officials in dismissing executive employees. On the same day the Supreme Court in another case ruled that the Attorney General could make no public listing of organizations declared to be communistic without affording them a hearing. "This is the first time," said Mr. Justice Jackson, "this court has held rights of individuals subordinate and inferior to those of organized groups. It is justice turned bottom-side up."

From the standpoint of recruitment for public employment, the question is not whether the loyalty program is legally sound but whether it is politically and administratively desirable. There can be no dissent from the preamble to Executive Order No. 9835 that "it is of vital importance that persons employed in the federal service be of complete and unswerving loyalty to the United States." At the same time, the government requires for the performance of its services the most capable and intelligent citizens obtainable. There has already been much criticism that government service tends largely to attract unimaginative men and women who lack the resources for any kind of work except routine tasks under supervision. While this criticism is unfair to thousands of public employees, it must be admitted that administrative policies which impose restraints upon the freedom of thought and expression will divert from government employment the very people whose loss can be least afforded. The dissenting opinion in *Bailey v. Richardson* remarked: "No doubt some [loyalty] boards are quite aware that unconventional views and conduct have no tendency to indicate disloyalty. But the fact remains that some boards imagine the contrary. This fact is only too well known. It puts government employees under economic and social pressure to protect their jobs and reputations by expressing in words and conduct only the most orthodox opinions on political, economic, and social questions."

The government of the United States and the governments of the eight or more states which have enacted laws requiring loyalty oaths already have ample statutory authority to refuse employment to persons who are guilty of disloyal conduct. Actions which are subversive in character can be punished readily under existing laws whether the perpetrators are already public employees or merely candidates for public employment. What the loyalty program seeks to accomplish is punishment for harboring thoughts which are disloyal and subversive. The development of administrative procedures which will accurately evaluate and appraise the thoughts of men has thus far defied human ingenuity.

It is a fantastic situation in which an organization is entitled to a judicial hearing before it can be branded as subversive while an employee can be removed and stigmatized as disloyal without being confronted by his accusers or being furnished with specific charges. The right to public employment is not drawn into question, because no such right exists. But the right to reputation is cherished by everybody. Unless the procedures of the loyalty program in federal and state governments can be so constructed that the reputations of loyal citizens will be adequately safeguarded, there will be little inducement for able and intelligent men and women to enter public employment.

Despite the obstacles to a career in government employment, thousands of men and women enter the civil service at federal, state, and local levels with the intention of remaining and advancing throughout a lifetime. The obstacles to advancement in public employment are not greater than in private enterprise. Of course, there is a distinction between a job and a career. No intelligent man will believe he can do more with a job than lay the foundations of a career. Whether in private industry or in public employment the chosen pursuit must lead to a measure of independence if the career is to be successful. In private enterprise a man will crown his career by going into business for himself. In public employment a man ought to aim at top-level administration. If by promotions and transfers he is unable to achieve this objective, he should leave the public service at the precise moment when his skills can command for him the greatest return in other markets. It is no more painful to separate oneself from a public payroll than to embark upon an independent business or profession. Anybody who is sincerely interested in a career must free himself from the limitations of time and place and do what is required to reach the higher levels of business or administration reasonably early in his lifetime. Those who tarry unduly long among the hewers of wood and drawers of water will not achieve a career; they will only hold a job.

CHAPTER II

THE PARADOX OF CIVIL SERVICE REFORM

CIVIL service reform in the United States aimed at the replacement of patronage appointments by selections on a basis of merit and fitness to be determined by competitive examinations. The attack upon the spoils system has succeeded in proportion to the vigor with which it has been pressed at all levels of government. The steady growth of the merit system at Washington and throughout the states testifies to the common sense and integrity of the American people. But the paradox of civil service reform is that the merit system has not at the same time created adequate standards of personnel administration. That is to say, the merit system has done much to recruit better people for public employment but seldom has helped the chief executive to gain control of the administration he is by law directed to perform.

The chief executive under our system of government is expected to provide political direction and political responsibility for administrative activities. The executive branch is organized so that the department heads can provide the vital elements of both political and administrative leadership for government operations. Most chief executives in federal and state governments have done a fair job in formulating public policy and obtaining legislative approval of the measures they have sponsored. They have just as often failed completely to influence the course of administration and to see that the objectives of the law are carried out. In other words, few chief executives discharge efficiently their obligation to take care that the laws be faithfully executed.

The Paradox of Civil Service Reform

The failure to develop sound standards of personnel administration is somewhat surprising in view of the responsibility of the chief executive for the conduct of the merit system. There can be no sound personnel administration under the merit system unless the chief executive understands and believes in its principles. The president, the governor, or the mayor must subscribe wholeheartedly to the principles of the merit system within his jurisdiction or the law becomes unavailing. A civil service law which lacks firm executive support soon becomes a cloak for the maintenance of a legalized spoils system.

Most chief executives have reached their positions through political training and achievements and many of them have accumulated heavy debts to party organizations in attaining victory at the polls. Almost nobody arrives at high office unaided. Executive responsibility for good personnel administration is frequently handicapped by promises of jobs to partisan supporters. It is a wise and capable chief executive who distinguishes carefully between positions available for patronage appointments and those protected by the merit system. Of course, failure to make this distinction and act upon it brings him into conflict with the law. But a great many chief executives have come perilously close to the brink of disaster as they have sought to chart a course between party obligations and the requirements of the civil service law.

The responsibility of the chief executive for the administration of the merit system has been a fundamental principle of civil service reform. Whenever the merit system has been adopted on any of the three levels of government in the United States, the administration of the system has been confided to the chief executive. Initially he has discharged this responsibility by the appointment of competent civil service commissioners or heads of personnel boards. But most civil service laws impose upon the chief executive a continuing responsibility for good personnel administration. He must approve the rules of civil service commissions, he must find the money with which to finance compensation plans, and he must defend the central personnel agency against the recurring attacks of enemies of the merit system. This exercise of executive responsibility will often bring a president, governor, or mayor into conflict not only with strongly entrenched interest groups but also with the leaders of his own political party. His only constant support will result from appeal to an enlightened electorate which recognizes the evils, nuisance and waste of the spoils system.

The adoption of measures of civil service reform in the United States involved departures from tradition in American politics. In the first place, reform was adopted initially by the federal government whence it spread to the states. There was no experimentation with the civil service at state levels before reforms were undertaken at Washington. In the second place, the reforms accomplished by the Pendleton Act in 1883 were not indigenous to this country but were borrowed from abroad. The palliative measures adopted by Congress before the Civil War did little to curb the abuses of the spoils system. It was not until Thomas Allen Jenckes of Rhode Island, after much correspondence with civil service reformers in England, brought forward his famous report of 1868 that the foundations were laid for the adoption of the merit system in this country.

Recognition of the evils in the spoils system did not lead immediately to curative measures but it did intensify study of what had been accomplished abroad.

The Paradox of Civil Service Reform

The remarkable analysis of civil service systems in Great Britain, China, France, and Prussia contained in the Jenckes Report was followed by an elaborate investigation of the British system by Dorman B. Eaton. At the request of President Hayes, Mr. Eaton visited England to study the new system of civil service introduced in 1870. He also investigated, at the request of the President, conditions in the New York customhouse and post office. Reports on both surveys were made available to Congress and provided civil service reformers with powerful weapons in their attack upon the spoils system.

Meanwhile, President Grant had approved as a rider to the appropriation bill introduced on March 3, 1871, a clause whereby "the President is authorized to prescribe such regulations for the admission of persons into the civil service of the United States as may best promote the efficiency thereof, and ascertain the fitness of each candidate in respect to age, health, character, knowledge and ability for the branch of the service into which he seeks to enter; and for this purpose he may employ suitable persons to conduct such inquiries, and may prescribe their duties, and establish regulations for the conduct of persons who may receive appointments in the civil service." By this act the application of the merit system was to be discretionary with the President, and he was to determine the conditions under which the system was to operate.

President Grant undertook to establish a merit system within the limits of the $25,000 appropriated by Congress in 1871. George William Curtis, a leader in civil service reform, became chairman of a board which later took the title of Civil Service Commission. He resigned in March 1873 and was succeeded as chairman by Dorman B. Eaton. But the hostility of Congress was soon aroused and in 1873 no new appropriation was made for the Civil Service Commission. Thereafter the Civil Service Commission continued in a shadowy sort of existence for ten years, although the reformers never relaxed in their efforts to secure support for their measures throughout the country and in Congress. The movement for civil service reform languished until the assassination of President Garfield.

President Garfield, exhausted by months of acrimonious dispute over the patronage, was about to leave Washington on July 2, 1881, for a visit to Williams College and a vacation with his family at Elberon, New Jersey, when he was shot down in the railway station by a disappointed office-seeker. As the martyred President lay dying at Elberon, a wave of sympathy swept over the country, and this was coupled with resentment against the patronage system. In the death of President Garfield civil service reform gained what it had been unable to achieve through the appeal to reason in Congress. Following the congressional elections of 1882, the members of Congress could no longer doubt the existence of a widespread popular demand for a reform of the civil service. Senator Pendleton of Ohio introduced a bill which had been prepared by Dorman B. Eaton, assisted by George William Curtis and other members of the National Civil Service Reform League. This bill, with modifications and additions, later became the Civil Service Act of 1883.

The Pendleton Act provided effective statutory authorization for the merit system. A civil service commission of three members, not more than two of whom should be adherents of the same political party, was to be appointed by the President by and with the advice and consent of the Senate. The commissioners were to aid the President in preparing rules to carry out the provisions of the law, and to make an annual report to the President for transmission to Congress describing the operation of the civil service system and suggesting means for the more effective accomplishment of the purposes of the act.

The civil service act further provides for open competitive examinations, practical in character, of applicants for the classified service; the making of appointments to the classified service from among those graded highest in the examinations; a probationary period before absolute appointment; and the apportionment of appointments to the departments at Washington according to the population of the states, territories, and the District of Columbia, as ascertained at the last preceding census. The appointment to the classified service of more than two members of one family is forbidden. Employees are safeguarded against demotion or dismissal for political reasons and against political assessments or enforced contributions to party funds. The political activity clauses of the civil service act have been supplemented by numerous executive orders and by the Hatch Act of August 2, 1939, and the amendments of July 19, 1940.

When the Pendleton Act became effective in 1883, the classified service included only 10.5 per cent of the executive civil service, or 13,900 positions. The growth of the classified service was steady but unimpressive until the administration of Theodore Roosevelt, who had been a member of the United States Civil Service Commission and who understood and believed in the merit system. Before he left the presidency, Theodore Roosevelt had brought many thousands of positions within the classified service until 63.9 per cent of the whole executive civil service was included. Thereafter, extensions of the classified service were made from time to time until the administration of President Hoover, when 80 per cent of the entire executive civil service had been brought within the provisions of the merit system.

The great economic depression ushered in by the stock market crash of 1929 laid unexpected burdens upon the government at Washington. For the first time in the history of the United States, millions of men and women were out of work and unable to find employment. Government at state and local levels failed to cope with the situation. Local relief organization collapsed completely under the strain of the greatly increased demand for public aid. The federal government was able to discharge the obligation thrust upon it to care for the unemployed only through a rapid and unprecedented increase in personnel. In order that the federal government might become "the great almoner of public charity throughout the United States," many thousands of new employees had to be added to the payroll. Since the emergency which dictated these new hirings was deemed to be purely temporary, the new employees were not embraced within the classified civil service. As a result of the addition of employees who were regarded as temporary, the percentage of positions within the classified service dropped abruptly in 1936 to 60.5, and the cry resounded everywhere that the civil service was being sabotaged in the interest of the political party then in power. The presidential campaign of 1936 was filled with charges and countercharges, and civil service reform was once more an issue at the polls.

The overwhelming success of the Democratic Party in the 1936 elections not only stifled the critics of the administration of Franklin D. Roosevelt but also restored confidence to the majority in the executive and legislative branches of the government. Civil service reform was transferred from the hustings to conference between

President Roosevelt and the majority leaders in Congress. In 1937 Congress continued to except many positions from the classified service but the next year began to abandon hostility to the merit system. The Ramspeck-O'Mahoney Postmaster Act and the executive orders issued by President Roosevelt on June 24, 1938, regained for the merit system much lost ground. The executive orders not only promulgated a complete revision of the civil service rules but also authorized the inclusion within the classified service of all federal positions, except those specifically excepted by statute and those of a policy-determining nature. In 1939 the enactment of the Ramspeck Act not only extended the classified service but also greatly improved the civil service under the merit system. Thus Congress joined with President Roosevelt at an opportune moment to bring about civil service reform. The net result of the legislation and the executive orders was to bring 72.5 per cent of the federal executive civil service within the merit system. On June 30, 1951, on a world-wide basis, 87.5 per cent of the employees in the executive civil service held appointments under the Commission's regulations; and in the continental United States 92.6 per cent held such appointments.

Civil service reform at Washington was followed by the adoption of the merit system in a few states. New York adopted a civil service law on May 4, 1883, and was followed the next year by Massachusetts. A lull ensued until 1905 when Illinois and Wisconsin joined the merit system states, to be followed closely by Colorado and New Jersey. By the end of World War I the merit system had been adopted in nine states. The most rapid advance has come since 1937 with the adoption by nine additional states of merit system laws covering all departments. Eighteen states now have civil service laws covering all departments while thirteen other states have one or more departments under some form of merit system in addition to those departments with merit system laws under the Social Security Act. In all states departments whose employees are paid wholly or in part from federal grants under the Social Security Act are required to be under a merit system. A number of states have anchored the merit system in the constitution by providing that appointments and promotions are to be made upon a basis of merit and fitness, to be determined, as far as practicable, by examination.*

Executive responsibility for the maintenance and development of the merit system in the federal government derives not only from the Pendleton Act but also from the rider to the appropriation act passed on March 3, 1871. This authorization to President Grant to ascertain the fitness of candidates for the civil service remains in effect today as Section 1753 of the Revised Statutes. Under its authority and that of the civil service act, the President issues civil service rules and other executive orders to govern the personnel of the executive civil service.

In the eighteen states which provide for general coverage within the merit system, all except Maryland have established civil service commissions or personnel boards. These are appointed by the governor for fixed

* I have relied upon statistical data obtained from the publication of the National Civil Service League, *Good Government*, LXVIII, pp. 1-6. A slightly different compilation of states having merit system provisions has been made by the Civil Service Assembly of the United States and Canada and is to be found in the *Book of the States, 1950-1951*, pp. 192-196, published by the Council of State Governments, Chicago, 1950. Figures showing the extent of the merit system among the municipalities of the United States will be found in the *Municipal Year Book*, Chicago, 1950, pp. 107 ff.

terms, usually with senate confirmation. Most of them are bipartisan, but this is not always required by law. The executive officer is ordinarily chosen for an indefinite term by the commission or personnel board, although in recent years some states have lodged this appointment directly in the governor. The executive officer is expected to be experienced in personnel administration and to supply the commission with technical advice. Ordinarily he administers the affairs of the central personnel agency.

Among the states where the merit system extends to all departments, there are, broadly speaking, five different forms of personnel control. When civil service reform was first undertaken in the states, complete authority was vested in civil service commissions. These commissions were entrusted with the administration of the civil service system as well as with the quasi-legislative and quasi-judicial powers appropriate to such agencies. In retrospect it is not difficult to understand why this type of civil service commission did not prove wholly successful. Almost none of the persons appointed to the commissions possessed any technical knowledge of personnel administration and nearly all of them received their appointments as rewards for political services. It is really surprising that civil service reform did not perish in its infancy in the hands of the commissions to which it was entrusted. Since 1920 the trend has been away from the amateur bipartisan civil service commission.

Some states have retained the civil service commission but have created a director of personnel or other executive officer who administers the civil service system. This executive officer is frequently chosen after a competitive examination and must be qualified in personnel administration. He brings to the department a technical knowledge of civil service matters almost never found among the commissioners. The division of authority between the commission and its executive officer has not always been satisfactory. The failure to define in law and practice the proper relationships between the commission and its executive officer has frequently led to confusion. The executive officer has lacked the authority and the responsibility necessary to carry out the administrative work of the department at the same time that the commission has not confined its activities to matters of policy, rule-making, and hearings. The result has been in most instances to handicap the executive officer in the conduct of routine departmental duties and to lay the members of the commission open to charges of irregular interference with the administration of the civil service system.

The third form of organization, to be found in a few states, seeks to avoid the division of authority and responsibility between the executive officer and the commission. There is created a personnel director flanked by an advisory committee with limited powers. Some advantages can be claimed in behalf of the advisory committee because it serves as a sounding board to test public reaction to proposed innovations in the civil service system. At the same time, it does not relieve the executive officer from the necessity of dealing directly with the governor and members of the legislature when they display anxiety about the filling of jobs.

Another modification of the traditional civil service commission has been attempted through the lodgment of greater powers in the president or head of the commission. This was undertaken in New Jersey in 1944 and was recommended for adoption in the federal government by the Hoover Commission on Organization of the Executive Branch of the Government in 1949. The extent to which the recommendations of the Hoover Commission were adopted is reflected in Reorganization Plan No. 5 of 1949, which became effective in August 1949. The title of the head of the United States Civil Service Commission is changed from "president" to "chairman." The responsibility for the administrative direction of the commission's operations is placed upon the chairman, although the three commissioners continue to be responsible for determination of policy and adjudication of appeals. The recent appointment of former Congressman Robert Ramspeck as chairman indicates the sincerity of President Truman's desire to provide sound administration for the federal civil service system although the civil service commission is retained.

The fifth form of organization is the single commissioner who administers the civil service system in Maryland. This complete break with established tradition has been praised but not followed in other jurisdictions. The President's Committee on Administrative Management in 1937 recommended the elimination of the United States Civil Service Commission and the appointment by the President of a non-political personnel director selected by means of a competitive professional examination. This examination would be supervised by a civil service board to be established on a per diem basis with only advisory and investigatory powers. The proposal of the President's Committee on Administrative Management was severely criticized on the ground that it placed in the hands of the President too much control over personnel. After a lapse of twelve years the Hoover Commission found to be inadequate the degree of control which the President has over the executive branch of the government—inadequate because of the lack of integration of personnel administration. Nevertheless, this commission was not prepared to recommend the elimination of the civil service commission and the substitution of the single commissioner as in Maryland.

The establishment in Maryland of a single commissioner to administer the merit system was wholly adventitious. The original bill prepared by advocates of civil service reform provided for an unpaid commission of three members who would have the power to appoint a secretary to perform such duties as might be prescribed. When the bill was submitted to the legislature in 1920 as an administration measure, it provided for a single state employment commissioner to be appointed by the governor for a term of six years. The bill was opposed in public hearings but Governor Ritchie succeeded in obtaining legislative approval without a single change in its provisions. Maryland thus obtained a thoroughly sound civil service law despite the opposition of the advocates of civil service reform.

In New Jersey the legislature in 1944 enacted a law reorganizing the civil service commission in an attempt to correct the evils arising from a division of authority between the commission and the executive officer, the chief examiner and secretary. This law provided that "all the executive functions, powers and duties vested in the commission . . . shall be performed, exercised or discharged, as the case may be, solely by the president." What this quaint phraseology means, nobody has taken the trouble to inquire. It plainly intended to subordinate the chief examiner and secretary to the president of the commission, from whom he received his appointment, and to exclude the commission from the exercise of any control or direction of the administration of the civil service system. The commission was left in the possession of the quasi-legislative and quasi-judicial functions set forth in the statute. Fortunately, the president of the commission first appointed under the act received the unfailing support of his colleagues as well as the chief examiner and secretary in supervising the civil service administration.

Whether the New Jersey innovations will lead to the establishment of sound civil service procedures in all likelihood depends upon the competence and integrity of the president of the civil service commission and the chief examiner and secretary. The other part-time salaried commissioners have few duties to perform, except the holding of hearings. They are excluded by the law so completely from the administration of the civil service system that they are unable to know its operations unless these are reported to them by the president. Since the commissioners are confined to very meager duties, the result may be that they will become focal points in the political pressures which strive for irregular interference in the administration of the civil service system. Unless some way can be found for the commissioners to participate in the promotion of the merit system more significantly than at present, it will become increasingly difficult to justify the expenditure of public funds for their salaries.

The Connecticut civil service law is generously praised by civil service reformers because it vests the appointment of the personnel director in the governor, and associates with him a commission in an advisory capacity. The personnel director is further strengthened in his administrative control over the civil service through membership on a personnel board with the governor and the commissioner of finance. This board determines all salaries except those of legislative and judicial employees. Appeals from employees who have been dismissed from their positions or otherwise disciplined are brought before a special appeals board. Whatever may be the merits of the Connecticut system, there can be no doubt that the governor has more direct and immediate control over personnel administration than is the case in most states under the merit system.

The time has passed when a civil service department can be maintained external to the administrative hierarchy without sacrificing much that is essential to good government. The emphasis in public employment has shifted from the exclusion of unqualified party workers to the inclusion of competent public employees. The problem is not so much that of "keeping the rascals out" as it is that of getting intelligent and capable men and women to accept public employment. In this shift of emphasis civil service reform has been only one factor. Much greater importance must be ascribed to increased skills required in the public services and to the need for economy in government. The new and more complex services being performed by government require qualified employees beyond the capacity of party organizations to provide. It would be very simple to hire qualified people to perform the public services and also retain the party workers "on the pad" if this did not increase the cost of government unduly. High tax rates and unreasonable assessments bring the scrutiny of taxpayers' associations, chambers of commerce, and other civic organizations into the structure of government as well as the public policies at all levels of government. Civil service reform is therefore required to enlarge the scope of its activities to include positive assistance to government in solving the problems of public employment.

"Fewer and better civil service employees" is a phrase in frequent use by public officials as well as civil service reformers without any clear indication of just what must be done either to reduce the number of employees or to increase the quality of those who remain. In the federal and state governments recent surveys have highlighted the subject of public payrolls in relation to the costs of government. How to make bureaucrats behave engaged the attention of the President's Committee on Administrative Management in 1937 and the Hoover Commission on Organization of the Executive Branch of the Government in 1949. Neither investigation resulted in a cure of the evils which both found to exist and which were diagnosed with skill and imagination. In the states the movement for administrative reorganization which began almost forty years ago has led to a multitude of surveys followed by numerous consolidations and readjustments. Some of these have been authorized by legislative enactments while others have sought firmer anchorage in constitutional provisions. The purpose in each case has been the same, to reduce the number of departments, boards, commissions, and agencies and to place each consolidated department under a responsible administrative head.

The tangible results of state administrative reorganization are somewhat less than could have been desired. In the first place, it cannot be said that the total costs of state government have anywhere been reduced by reorganization and consolidation. That is not the fault of reorganization. The people have been asking more and more services at the state level and have demanded that these be performed by the state government. Highways, health, welfare, teacher-training, and a host of other services have been thrust upon the state governments and have had to be supported by state funds. There is no end of this expansion in sight. It must be expected, therefore, that state budgets will grow in size. What can be said with some degree of confidence is that the costs of government would have been higher if reorganization had not been undertaken.

In the second place, the power of the governor, particularly over the distribution of the patronage, has been greatly increased through reorganization. As everybody knows, in the early days of the American political system a profound distrust of the office of governor existed throughout the country. This distrust has been overcome because the pressure of circumstances has left the governor as the only effective leader in the state government. While reorganization has increased the control of the governor over the patronage, almost no governor has availed himself of this power to exact good administration from his department heads. The governor can and does function as a partisan political patronage broker distributing the offices available to him under the law as rewards to persons who have rendered service to the party. At this point his interest in administration wanes and he leaves untouched the great army of civil service employees while he turns to the politically more remunerative task of securing the adoption of his legislative proposals.

The lack of administrative skill and experience among American chief executives extends to all levels of government. No President in recent years, except Hoover, and few governors have had much experience with the administration of large affairs before taking office. They have as a rule been chosen because of their availability to the party rather than their fitness as administrators. The American *cursus honorum* is not designed to bring to high office great administrators. Its Roman prototype embraced rules which required years of military experience before political office could be held. There was also a degree of seasoning required in subordinate offices before the ranks of higher magistracy could be reached. In the United States the experience prior to taking high office is ordinarily not with administration but with political tactics guided by party organization.

The preoccupation of the American chief executive with legislative programs is not without compensation. It does compel a degree of high-level planning for the results of which the political party can be held to account. Administrative bungling will sooner or later receive legislative attention and perhaps party discipline. The alternative to ascent to high office through party service is usually provided by reform movements whose candidates succeed because of widespread popular resentment against the party organization. In this way there may be tossed into prominence grotesque nonentities and incapables who never could have obtained important office by the ordinary gradation of political preferment. The American people are wisely not stampeded into reform movements outside the regular party organizations for light and transient causes. They usually prefer to seek the cure of evils arising from bad administration by entrusting the government to the party of opposition at the next election.

While structural changes in the government may be required to perfect public administration, a great deal of improvement would result from a return to the original principles of civil service reform. Historically the merit system was introduced to supersede the spoils system. That is to say, appointments to jobs were to be on a basis of merit and fitness, and protection against dismissal for political, racial, or religious reasons was guaranteed. Security of tenure was not intended to protect incompetence or misconduct. The appointing authority was not to be restricted in the internal operations of his department by the adoption of the merit system. Rather what he must do is to make his appointments from civil service eligible lists. What he must not do is to discriminate among his employees on political, racial, or religious grounds. It was never the purpose of the merit system to transfer to the central personnel agency the control of public employees so that the heads of operating departments lost their authority effectively to deal with them.

The security afforded by a civil service system is not against loss of employment. The safeguard of any civil service law consists in a set of rules binding upon appointing authorities as well as employees. When structural or administrative changes are in contemplation by any government, the rights of civil service employees are to the exercise of certain procedures set forth in the law. Compliance with these procedures was never intended to paralyze the policy-making branches of the government from proceeding with changes required in the interest of improved public services.

What a civil service law contemplates is that a new policy when adopted shall take into account old employees. When old employees are displaced as a result of administrative reorganizations, they should be given reemployment opportunities as vacancies in comparable positions arise. They should not again be required to compete in civil service tests for the same or similar positions to which they were once appointed. When the same or a similar position has been recreated, the incumbent under civil service laws and regulations of a position which has been abolished has the first call on the new appointment.

Unfortunately a minority of civil service employees or their spokesmen have forgotten the basic principles of the merit system. Employee leaders have frequently perverted the security of tenure under civil service laws to assert in behalf of a civil service appointee an indefeasible right to a job and its emoluments, and to oppose any governmental alterations which affect adversely the employee. Lay-offs, reductions in force, the abolition of unnecessary positions, and the consolidation of services in the interest of economy are always fruitful sources of complaint. The stand-pat attitude of an organized group of public employees will often deter legislators from embarking upon governmental changes highly desirable from the point of view of the general welfare. Recognition of this propensity to regard public employment as a vested right cropped out in the discussions of the Civil Service Assembly of the United States and Canada at San Francisco in 1949. It was clear to all whose professional interest lies in the maintenance and advancement of the merit system that a doctrine of vested right as applied to public jobs is both ridiculous and dangerous.

Some public employees spend a great part of their time not in the conduct of the public business but in demonstrating that the continuance of their jobs is absolutely essential to the functioning of the American political system. They appear to subscribe to what might be called "pushpin" politics, to borrow a term from 17th century English political theory. That is to say, they believe that not a pin can be removed from government lest the whole edifice fall into ruin. The particular pin which must not be removed is that which fastens the employee to the payroll. While it is desirable that public employees be impressed by the importance of their work, the decision as to whether the particular duties shall continue to be performed cannot safely be entrusted to anybody except the political heads of the government. A real danger arises when the selfish interests of jobholders are permitted to intrude upon the deliberations of governmental policy.

The clannishness of civil service employees is frequently displayed in the defense of incumbents who have been dismissed for incompetence or misbehavior. The pithy advice attributed to the late Senator Boies Penrose of Pennsylvania to "stand by your own damn rascals" is heeded by civil service employees as well as politicians. In a recent case the appointing authority in a reformatory for women requested a male employee to vacate his quarters on the grounds of the institution although he was continued in his employment. To anyone of discernment this request would have appeared so reasonable that it would have received immediate compliance. But the civil service employee with the support of his fellow-workers alleged a grievance and demanded a hearing. At this point the county prosecutor was invited to make an investigation with the result that the employee was indicted on fourteen counts and convicted of misconduct in court.

It may be argued that arbitrary and high-handed conduct by department heads has compelled civil service employees to stick together. The fact remains that good employees seldom get into trouble. Every department head knows that he will be held responsible for the prompt and efficient performance of the public services entrusted to him. Even those political heads who have nothing to recommend them except slavish attention to party activities will hesitate to remove civil service employees unless the reasons for the removal are sound and in the public interest. What more often happens is that incompetent and misbehaving employees are continued on the payroll because the task of dismissing them is too great to be undertaken. The appointing authority, burdened with the duties of his office, shrinks from the unpleasantness which attends a dismissal. Statistics have been compiled to show that the dismissal rate in state and local governments has been slightly lower than the current discharge rate in private industry. At the same time, the dismissing authorities have been upheld by civil service agencies in more than 95 per cent of the cases which have been appealed. The record will not support the employee claim that public officials are harsh and capricious in the maintenance of discipline within their departments or agencies. What is more certainly revealed is the need for summary action in dealing with unfit employees. The safeguards which surround civil service employees should not be extended to protect incompetence and misbehavior.

The most serious indictment of civil service employees stems from their opposition to increased educational requirements for public employment. There was a time when the grammar school could provide the necessary training for most civil service positions. This was followed by the requirement that candidates for many positions be graduates of high schools. With the increasing complexity of government services there has arisen a large number of positions for which a college training is required. In a great many civil service jurisdictions the most persistent opposition to higher educational qualifications has developed on the part of employees already in the system. These people realize that they are denied opportunities for promotion when educational levels beyond which they have not progressed are set for civil service examinations. The California State Employees' Association and some of the trade unions have met this situation by providing facilities for the training of their members. But most civil service groups as well as many individuals have attacked the higher educational qualifications. They protest to civil service commissions, threaten litigation, and otherwise exhibit an uncompromising opposition to all efforts to improve the civil service through greater requirements of formal education. Sometimes they succeed for a time in compelling the evaluation of experience with formal education. In this way civil service departments are often obliged to grant credits for routine experience in the service in lieu of professional qualifications. The result is a general weakening of the government service to pave the way for the promotion of the unqualified. There can be no strong and vigorous civil service where the employees are permitted to have a hand in determining the qualifications for admission or promotion.

Civil service reform has a paramount obligation to uphold the ideal of merit and fitness for appointments and promotions in the public service. The requirement of merit and fitness applies not only at the time of original appointment but also throughout the service of the employee. The merit system does not discharge its obligation to the people unless it provides for the elimination of the unfit as well as the appointment of the meritorious. It is unfortunate but inevitable in any government that men and women will receive appointments to jobs to the requirements of which they are unable to adjust. Other civil service employees will undergo such deterioration of character in the course of their employment that their dismissal becomes the only remedy to ensure proper performance of the services of government. These are in a sense the failures of the system, but like all failures they demand corrective measures. The civil service system will not command widespread respect and support if it permits groups of employees to strive for the retention on the payroll of persons of demonstrated unfitness.

The public employees had little or nothing to do with the introduction of the merit system in the United States. They were the immediate beneficiaries of a system which was designed to elevate the moral tone of government and secure greater economy and efficiency in the operation of the public services. The advocates of the merit system were the enlightened leaders of public opinion who organized the early civil service reform associations. The agitation has been carried on over a period of seventy years by men and women of education, wealth, and social position. Their efforts have succeeded largely because of the non-partisan character of the movement and the candor with which its aims have been presented to the people. Civil service reform would long since have failed if the electorate had believed that the merit system would come to shelter selfish minorities of public employees who seek to subvert its principles in behalf of excessive job protection. The merit system thrives because the electorate, including an overwhelming majority of the civil service employees, are convinced, in the jurisdictions where it has been adopted, that its principles ensure more economical and efficient government. The same straightforward policy pursued in securing the adoption of the merit system can be counted upon to effect its preservation.

Civil service reform has not yet exhausted the possibilities which it once contained for the improvement of public employment. It is still possible for civil service reformers to offer a constructive service equal to that provided by George William Curtis, Dorman B. Eaton, and the pioneers of the National Civil Service Reform League. What the modern reformers must undertake is nothing less than the reconciliation of the principle of merit and fitness for appointment and promotion in the civil service with the requirement that the chief executive shall at all times be able to control the amount and quality of the administration for which he is by law responsible. In other words, the chief executive at federal, state, and local levels must be enabled to utilize the personnel under the merit system to the best advantage to accomplish the efficient purposes of government. There are already indications that this problem has been thoroughly grasped, although an adequate solution has not yet been found.

The Hoover Commission found that the executive branch of the federal government is not organized into a workable number of major departments and agencies which the President can effectively direct, but is cut up into a large number of agencies, which divide responsibility and which are too great in number for effective direction from the top. Clearly the President cannot personally direct thousands of programs, but there are at present a large number of agencies subject to no direction except that of the President. Mr. Hoover and his associates believe that the first step necessary to secure sound administration is to group federal programs according to related functions and assign them to departments the heads of which are directly responsible to the President. The second step is to bring all the dispersed agencies presently responsible to the President into subordination to an appropriate department head.

The authority of the President having been established to function through department heads, it becomes necessary that the line of command and supervision from the President down through his department heads to every employee, and the line of responsibility from each employee of the executive branch to the President, shall be clearly outlined. This line of responsibility has always existed in constitutional theory, but in practice it has been worn away by detailed statutory provisions, political pressures, and administrative practices. The task to which Mr. Hoover and his associates directed attention requires congressional action to remove statutory obstacles to presidential management of the executive branch.

The report of the Hoover Commission remarks that the federal government has not taken aggressive steps to build a corps of administrators of the highest level of ability with an interest in the program of government as a whole. Positive steps to make more attractive a career in the federal service include provisions for higher salaries and more practical programs for the promotion of competent employees. It is the duty of any civil service commission to prevent competent men and women in the civil service from becoming stymied in "dead end" jobs. The civil service commission will often have to battle with the civil service employees themselves in order to introduce qualitative selection among public personnel. There can be no doubt that the requirements of a sound personnel program demand that the civil service commission be enabled to spend a large amount of time and money in facilitating the transfer of competent career people from one agency to another. Coupled with a workable scheme of transfers there must be practical programs of promotion for qualified employees. Every civil service employee is entitled to be considered at some time for advancement, but that is not to say that everyone who succeeds in passing a test at the entrance level should be regarded as a candidate whenever a promotion is to be made. A civil service system fails if it cannot sift out and advance as rapidly as possible the good employees. Through the emphasis which it has placed upon the necessity for more intelligent and capable civil service employees the Hoover Commission has pointed the way to an improved merit system at the same time that it has sought to strengthen the control of the President over administrative management.

The Paradox of Civil Service Reform

There is one recommendation of importance which lies deeply buried in the report of the task force on the improvement of departmental management to the Hoover Commission. This report states: "We believe that a standard practice should now be introduced in the federal government whereby the heads of the subordinate operating units of a department are selected by the department heads on a merit basis. At the same time we believe that the department head should be free to dismiss any bureau chief with whom he is unable to collaborate effectively. The bureau chief might then be assigned to some other position in the department or even in another department. The merit system should not be used to perpetuate in major departmental positions individuals who are unwilling to accept the general direction of, or unable to satisfy the responsible political official of a department. Under the present circumstances there is too often a disposition on the part of bureau chiefs to intrigue against department heads. Career employees of government should have work security but not a lien on any specific job." The issue at bottom is one of loyalty to the government. A policy which has been decided by the responsible heads of the government must not be thwarted in its execution by some career employee who does not agree with the policy. To permit interference of this kind by dissatisfied civil service employees is no less destructive of good government than the nurture of subversive elements in public employment. The successful operation of any system of government requires that policy changes be reflected promptly and surely in the system of administration. Totalitarian forms of government gain their administrative ends without interference or delay. It is not less important in a democracy that decisions reached on the policy-making level be accorded firm and speedy execution.

In state and local governments the adaptation of the merit system to the requirements of strong executive control will be helped by pondering the recommendations of the Hoover Commission. While Mr. Hoover was concerned solely with the improvement of the government at Washington, the principles of public personnel administration set forth in his report are applicable with modifications at all levels of government. It is just as important to good administration in the states and larger municipalities that there be executive responsibility for the direction of an intelligent and capable civil service as in the federal government. Many governors are interested to make a record of substantial accomplishments chiefly as a platform on which to campaign for further political advancement. By requiring that good administration become a necessary prerequisite for political preferment, a governor will be obliged to look beyond the acceptance of his legislative proposals. When he is obliged to satisfy the requirements of political life by carrying out efficiently the legislative enactments he has sponsored, a governor will have justified his own further advancement. Good administration is impossible without an adequate control of the civil service.

The ultimate survival of the merit system in public employment depends upon its alliance with the requirements of sound administrative management. Where the merit system has been given a fair trial no responsible person would today argue for a return to an unrestricted spoils system. The principle of merit and fitness in appointments and promotions in the public service is firmly established. But neither the politicians nor the electorate will long tolerate the maintenance of a sinister interest of public employees fortified behind a civil service system and seeking to thwart the purpose of government. Intelligent political leaders welcome the merit system as a means of keeping the lower echelons of the party in line. The necessity of passing a civil service examination for public employment relieves the party leaders of making choices which are invidious. At the same time, the merit system reassures the intelligent and highminded citizens that competent men and women are being selected for government jobs. There remains to be solved the problem of strengthening the authority of the chief executive so that he is enabled to place the civil service employees advantageously for the performance of the services of government.

The cooperation of groups such as the National Civil Service League with intelligent public officials and party leaders is required not only to defend the merit system against attack but also to make it useful in administrative management. This partnership of civil service reformers and leaders in politics and government calls for understanding and forbearance on both sides. The advocates of civil service reform must lift their sights and broaden their horizons to embrace the whole governmental process. It is not enough that people of merit and fitness be employed in government. Their continued employment must be justified solely by the needs of government for their services. Tenure in an unwanted or unnecessary position is a waste of public funds. The aims of civil service reforms should therefore be identical with that of economy and efficiency in government.

Public officials must strive to understand and believe in the principles of the merit system. They must be willing to make their appointments according to the rules and regulations of the civil service commission or central personnel agency and not according to the dictates of party policies. This they must do in the confident expectation that they will thereby obtain better qualified employees than they could secure through any patronage scheme. When civil service reform is undertaken as a joint enterprise of reformers, public officials, and party leaders, it will become a powerful instrument for the improvement of government.

CHAPTER III

EMPLOYER-EMPLOYEE RELATIONSHIPS

FEW problems of public employment are more important than those of the relationships between public officials and the employees of government. These must lead to a genuine partnership if the services of government are to be efficiently performed. Distinctions between management and employees may be required at times in order to get the work done, but both parties must regard themselves as servants of the people. Because of the public interest which clothes their positions, they are under obligation to conduct themselves not as buyers and sellers of labor but as joint proprietors in the work of government which has been entrusted to them.

The importance of employer-employee relationships was not fully perceived in the early stages of the civil service system. With the same impractical outlook which characterized much of nineteenth century liberalism, the civil service reformers believed that they had solved all the problems of public personnel administration when they had secured the adoption of the merit system. They failed to recognize that whenever people come in contact in the struggles of life there is friction, and they did nothing to relieve the tensions which arise among civil service employees. Recruitment on a basis of merit and fitness, security of tenure, and protection against dismissal for racial, religious, or political reasons were thought to embrace all the requirements of a perfect system of public personnel. Adequate salaries, reasonable hours of work, sick leaves and vacations, retirement allowances, decent working conditions including proper equipment, and opportunities to suggest improvements in departmental operations were not mentioned. In other words, a great many legitimate interests of civil service employees fell outside the provisions of the civil service laws and have remained incapable of inclusion within the normal jurisdiction of civil service departments.

The neglect of important interests of public employees in the civil service laws and regulations was accompanied by attempts to impose political neutrality upon the service. The so-called "gag order" of President Theodore Roosevelt in 1902 forbade federal employees to seek to influence legislation in their own behalf "individually or through associations, except through the heads of their departments." For more than a decade federal employees complained against the restrictions imposed upon them by administrative officials. Unrest, defiance, threats, and strikes among government employees culminated in 1912 in the passage of the Lloyd-LaFollette Act which removed the administrative restrictions prohibiting government employees individually or collectively from petitioning Congress. For the enactment of this legislation the federal employees were heavily indebted to the American Federation of Labor.

The interest of the American labor movement in public employees has resulted in the growth of trade unions at every level of government. Both the American Federation of Labor and the Congress of Industrial Organizations sponsor unions in the states, counties, and municipalities as well as the federal government. There are also numerous unaffiliated unions. To these must be added the craft unions organized wholly among government employees or including the employees of both government and private enterprise. The extent of union organization throughout the United States cannot be accurately tabulated, although their history has been adequately recounted. There is abundant evidence that union membership has been steadily increasing. If the unions had devoted some of the time and energy expended in recruitment to the development of appropriate procedures through which to benefit their members, the problem of employer-employee relationships would today be nearer solution. Unfortunately, the impact of trade unionism upon government, especially at state and local levels, has been imperfectly understood. In many jurisdictions neither public officials nor union leaders have approached the settlement of differences through timely and intelligent negotiations.

In the first place, there has not been unanimous agreement among trade unionists on the methods to be pursued in handling the issues that arise in public employment. Mr. Samuel Gompers, who did much in the years before World War I to promote the organization of public employees in trade unions, subsequently became convinced that the sovereign employer would always be in a position to assert its claims over the men and women on government payrolls. In other words, Mr. Gompers recognized that the rights and privileges extended to government employees were precariously held at the pleasure of the sovereign employer. He therefore argued before the American Federation of Labor at Montreal in 1920 against the nationalization of railroads and in support of the individual liberties of American workers. His position was that industrial freedom required resistance to the expansion of governmental activity although this involved curtailment of the growth of public employment.

Mr. Gompers perceived correctly that trade union methods would be jeopardized when opposed by governmental authority entrenched behind the law. The expansion of governmental activity did not halt, but neither did the American Federation of Labor adapt its procedures to the requirements of public employment. Within a decade after the death of Mr. Gompers the leading union of federal employees, the National Federation of Federal Employees, severed its connection with the American Federation of Labor. The cause for the rupture was the inability of the majority in the American Federation of Labor to understand the special problems of a union in public employment. When these conflicted with the interests of the bulk of the membership in the American Federation of Labor, the federal employees found it necessary to withdraw and become an independent union.

Some leaders of craft unions have asserted that the American labor movement should withdraw from the public field because of its inability to function therein through normal trade union methods. The closed shop is impossible and the union shop is impracticable under any civil service system. In private industry, under the practice enforced by the National Labor Relations Board and by similar boards in a number of states, the representatives of the majority voting were given exclusive "recognition." The Taft-Hartley Labor-Management Relations Act added a new provision which permits any employee or group of employees to present grievances to their employer and to have such grievances adjusted, without the intervention of the bargaining representative, as long as the adjustment is not inconsistent with the terms of a collective-bargaining agreement then in effect. In public employment the collective-bargaining agreement has no such legal protection. It has no firmer foundation than the promise of the political official who made it. Fears have been expressed by some trade unionists that the inclusion of collective-bargaining agreements in a relationship wherein they are legally meaningless may result in great harm to the procedures of organized labor. When it is discovered that collective-bargaining agreements in public employment are idle gestures their strength in private industry may come to be impaired.

In the second place, many public officials have taken refuge behind the impressive legal bulwarks which surround their offices and have refused to recognize the unions as representatives of the public employees. Department heads can and often do refuse to deal with the employees under their jurisdiction and are sometimes reluctant to listen to their complaints. The political head does not depend for continuance in office upon the success with which he administers his department but upon the contribution which he is able to make to the aims of his party. The bounds and limits of his authority are circumscribed by the law and the exercise of his discretion is measured by the exigencies of party programs. No department head will refuse to comply with the law, but he can and often will decline to carry out agreements if changing circumstances make it politically undesirable for him to redeem a promise.

While the administrative official cannot be fettered in the exercise of his discretion, he can be directed by law to receive and consider petitions and complaints from public employees. The right of petition is inherent in the American philosophy of government and is sometimes spelled out in constitutional provisions. It is but a slight step from the right of petition to the negotiation of differences in public employment, but it is a step which is not always taken. The results of a recent survey of more than one thousand strikes among government employees indicate that the real reason for many work stoppages was arbitrary and high-handed conduct on the part of the public official to whom a request was presented. What the public has been told in a great many cases was that the employees had gone on strike for higher wages. The truth of the matter has usually been that the employees struck because they could get no consultation with the governmental authority to discuss the question of higher wages. The record appears to show that public employees are most unlikely to quit work as long as they are free to consult with their department heads about the issues which divide them.

The refusal to discuss a grievance is a greater injury to the public employee than the denial of his claim. Intransigence on the part of public officials harms the government as well as the employees. It leads to situations such as the strike of sanitation employees in Newark, New Jersey, in 1942, although similar incidents have occurred elsewhere.

An agreement was made between the Director of Public Works, city of Newark, and Local 277 of the State, County, and Municipal Workers of America (CIO) which contained the usual provisions for consultation and the establishment of procedures for the handling of grievances. In October 1941 the union voted to request a wage increase of 15 cents an hour and presented the request to the director. According to the brief of the union, the director on February 2, 1942, refused to consider any wage increase and thereafter declined to receive representatives of the union for consultation as provided in the agreement. After vainly endeavoring to talk with the director, the union appealed to Governor Edison and the National War Labor Board. Neither the Governor nor the War Labor Board was able to afford any redress and the union called a strike. The work stoppage lasted six days and involved about four hundred employees. The strike ended with the dismissal or prolonged suspension of about fifty-five employees, including the leaders of the union.

Since the city of Newark had been for thirty years under state civil service law, the dismissed and suspended employees appealed to the New Jersey State Civil Service Commission for reinstatement. In upholding the Newark municipal authorities, the Commission said:

"The issues in this case are clear. They extend beyond the question of the complete accuracy of minute details of time and place and conversations, and even beyond the question of whether the Director of the Department of Public Works has been able to hold the scales in even balance throughout the whole of these proceedings at every step taken and in every decision made. They involve directly the integrity and force of the law, the authority of municipal government administered by the elected officials of the people, whether public employees charged with duties affecting the public health and well-being are amenable to the laws and authority governing their employment, and whether they have the right to strike in an effort to enforce their demands upon a department or agency of the government in which they are employed. . . .

"There is no claim that these appellants or any other employees were required to work beyond their strength, that the hours of work were unreasonably long or that the conditions under which they were required to work were dangerous and intolerable. The testimony and the whole record in this case indicate that these employees were seeking to lay down the terms and conditions under which they would work and to fix, or to have a determining voice in fixing, the hours they would work and the pay which they should receive. In defense of their action the appellants stress the fact that the director of the department would not go into conference with them or grant them hearings and that he would not agree to mediation of the demands made upon him which, on the testimony of their representatives, did not get beyond the matter of wages. . . .

"Public employees have their rights as do other citizens, but in the very nature of their employment they must forego some of the practices which private employees may exercise while they remain as public employees, in return for tenure and other protective features assured them in their employment and for the public good. The civil service law was enacted by the elected representatives of the people of this state in recognition and consideration of these facts. Public employees are free to organize for the advancement of their common legitimate interests. They have the right to choose their own representatives to present to the proper authorities what they may determine to be their proper interests, but the public interest is always paramount. The government is the people. Public employees are a part of the government which they serve. Government must have sufficient authority to insure its continuity and the discharge of its essential services without interruption, otherwise it becomes impotent and its very existence is threatened. Public employees may confer and discuss and bargain collectively with respect to certain matters affecting their welfare, but collective bargaining in its full meaning as it applies to private employees is not applicable to the public service. A single department or agency of government is not the whole government. The head of such department or agency is limited in both his legal and administrative authority and action. He cannot bargain with individuals or groups involving expenditures beyond the budgetary limits of his department or set up plans and rates whose effect would extend to other departments and agencies of the government.

In the instant case the whole Board of City Commissioners alone has the authority to provide expenditures in any department or agency beyond budgetary limits and it is definitely limited in such action by statute, by current revenues and by state supervision. . . .

"There is no place in the whole scheme of government in this state for the settlement of differences which may arise between groups of departmental employees and the legally constituted officials in charge of such departments by way of strike. The acceptance of the right to strike by civil service employees would nullify the civil service law itself with all its beneficial effects. The acceptance of the right to strike would take away the authority of legally constituted public officials to administer government for the people. It would be a constant and impending threat upon the continuity and the authority of government itself."

The paramount public interest was vindicated in the Newark decision but at great cost to the morale of the municipal employees. The garbage collectors returned to work but the burning sense of injustices which permeated the municipal service was not removed. This would have been an opportune moment to establish through legislation appropriate procedures for the settlement of disputes through negotiations from which neither public officials nor employees could withdraw until some adjustment had been reached. Nothing of this kind has been done in New Jersey. Elsewhere the trend in legislation has been not toward the development of new procedures for the settlement of issues between the officers of government and the employees but in the direction of the prohibition of strikes. In other words, the sovereign employer has chosen coercion rather than conciliation.

The prohibition against strikes in the public service has been highlighted by its inclusion in the Taft-Hartley

Act. Section 305 of this legislation prohibits strikes by federal employees in the following terms:

"It shall be unlawful for any individual employed by the United States or any agency thereof including wholly owned government corporations to participate in any strike. Any individual employed by the United States or by any such agency who strikes shall be discharged immediately from his employment, and shall forfeit his civil service status, if any, and shall not be eligible for reemployment for three years by the United States or any such agency."

At the same time, a number of the states have enacted anti-strike laws applying to state employees, these laws being based upon the assumption that there are inherent differences in the conditions of public and private employment. The Condon-Wadlin Act in New York is the most drastic of all these laws. The act forbids strikes by all employees of the state and its political subdivisions. In addition to the loss of his job, any striking employee who is returned to his employment is prohibited for a period of three years from receiving more pay than he got at the time he went on strike. Finally, strikers who are reemployed are to be placed on probation for five years after they return to work, during which time they are subject to summary discharge. The law applies with equal force to individuals who absent themselves from their positions without leave as it does to groups of employees who have declared a strike. In other words, the unauthorized absence of an individual employee is deemed to be a strike.

The federal and state laws prohibiting strikes of public employees are based upon a faulty assumption. They assume that public and private employment are so different in nature that public employees must be isolated from other men and women and be subjected to special disabilities in order that the public services may not be disrupted. A work stoppage is regarded as a defiance of government itself which the sovereign employer must repress as it would an insurrection. In the light of the great increase in governmental activities it becomes impossible to distinguish in this way between public and private employment. There is no justification for keeping public employees at work by prohibiting strikes that would not apply equally to large areas of employment in private enterprise.* In either case employees quit their jobs because grievances are not redressed. The remedy will not be found in repressive measures but through conscientious efforts to remove the causes for the grievances.

The lack of wisdom displayed by these anti-strike laws is all the more amazing because they ignore the lessons which should have been learned from civil service reform. The early advocates of the merit system believed that they could neutralize politically the civil service employees. In other words, they saw the public employees as a class of political eunuchs. But the men and women on civil service payrolls continued to exhibit a lively interest in their own welfare. They accepted the benefits of the merit system and then demanded that attention be given to their legitimate interests not comprehended within civil service laws. Despite repressive measures, civil service employees individually and in groups have voiced to the politicians their complaints. No evil was ever cured by forbidding people to talk about it.

* A strong case can be made for the prohibition of strikes among patrolmen and firemen. The subject of police unionism is ably discussed by Sterling D. Spero, *Government As Employer*, New York, 1948, Chapter 12.

Anti-strike laws tend to destroy the ideal of partnership in the operation of government which is essential to the proper functioning of democratic institutions. Happiness is particularly important in government service because of the relations between the employees and the public. A majority of government employees, especially at state, county, and municipal levels, are brought into direct contact with the public, while few employees of private concerns, outside retail and service businesses, have contacts beyond their fellow employees. The public employee must therefore not only have a thorough knowledge of the tasks he performs but must also be able to maintain good relations with the public and must be ready at all times to justify the correctness of his actions to that portion of the public with whom he deals. In the last analysis, the success or failure of any government depends largely upon the loyalty of the men and women who perform its services. Loyalty is not a product of coercive measures.

The problem of employer-employee relationships in the public service can be solved only by patient negotiation among all parties concerned. It transcends questions of title, salary ranges, and other matters confided by law to civil service agencies. Many of the details of this problem cannot be brought within the terms of a specific statute, although all of them should be capable of solution through sympathetic cooperation between department heads and employees. The conditions of work in government departments, the shortcomings of management and of employees, the adequacy of facilities for the conduct of departmental operations and the continued well-being of public employees are all proper questions for discussion among employees and department heads and for remedial action.

It is precisely because the officers and employees of

government have an identity of interests that the problem of employer-employee relationships becomes capable of solution through negotiation. It lends itself to professional, scientific study just as completely as any other social or political problem. The department head who is worth his salt will welcome proposals for the betterment of his department whether these are made by individuals or by organized groups of employees. A wise department head will make certain that there is machinery set up for regular and continuous discussion of common problems with the employees under his jurisdiction. The outcome of these discussions should be the solution of most of the problems. Where the solution agreed upon transcends the existing law, recommendations in form suitable for legislative action should be made to the chief executive and the legislature. Sometimes the satisfaction of just demands will require increased appropriations. When budget increases are necessary, the taxpayers should be clearly informed and public officials and employees should agree upon the representations to be made to the public.

Honest differences of opinion may sometimes arise between department or agency heads and the public employees. These deadlocks should not terminate negotiations but only transfer them to some impartial tribunal where the paramount public interest may pronounce a final decision. The issues upon which the officers and employees of government fail to agree are not union matters nor are they wholly the concern of the department head. They are of public concern. The people as well as the department heads and public employees have a right to expect that these controversies shall be settled expeditiously and finally through some agency of the government. In other words, there must be some competent scheme of arbitration.

Arbitration has not been as readily accepted in public employment as it has in the settlement of labor disputes in private industry. This is not the fault of the unions. From the record it would appear that civil service unions have generally been willing to submit their claims to "outside" arbitration while the reluctance to arbitrate has been on the side of the public officials. Many times the officers of government have refused to submit differences to arbitration on the ground that they could not in this way abdicate their authority over the employees responsible to them. On the other hand, there have been numerous instances in the federal government where advisory arbitrations have been accepted by department and agency heads.

Although arbitration has particular advantages in the interpretation and application of a collective agreement already in force, it need not be confined to such circumstances. Unions have repeatedly requested the submission of wage and other disputes to public arbiters where there was no collective-bargaining agreement in existence. Local 504 of the SCMWA (CIO) in Trenton, New Jersey, had no agreement in 1945 when it offered to submit its entire case for wage increases to arbitration by a panel to be appointed by the New Jersey State Civil Service Commission. The municipal authorities declined to accept arbitration and the leaders of the union subsequently decided to call a strike. What the union sought was an impartial consideration of its claims before a body representative of the public interest. It is no argument to say that the public officials are themselves the representatives of the people. They have been given no mandate to conduct public affairs by exploiting the employees. The public employees are just as much representatives of the people within the limitations of their positions, but they have no right to press unreasonable demands upon the elected and appointive officials. When differences between officers and employees of government will not yield to settlement through negotiation, they should be submitted to an impartial arbitration under conditions carefully defined by law.

There are admitted limitations to the use of arbitration in public employment. The awards of an arbitration panel cannot be final if they exceed the authority vested in the administrator. They cannot supplant the public power itself. This is generally recognized. The area within which finality can be claimed for an award by arbitration is that bounded by the discretion of the administrator. But the decision of an impartial arbiter can become a powerful force in securing changes in the law or alterations in a budget. It can be submitted to the people as the basis for a referendum measure. While there are dangers to be avoided in the use of the machinery of arbitration, the chances of ultimate success greatly outweigh the likelihood of failure.

A more thorny question arises in the determination of what form of employee association is best adapted to public employment. The unions have in many jurisdictions been obliged to compete with independent civil service associations. It would be a hardy theorizer who undertook to select any particular organization as the best form of association. While trade unions and independent civil service associations subscribe to the merit system, both are at times disposed to pursue tactics which tend to undermine the principle of merit and fitness for appointments and promotions in the civil service. The competition among different organizations leads some of them to demand the administration of the civil service system according to their own preconceived notions rather than the provisions of the law.

Employer-Employee Relationships

In spite of the conflicting opinions which emanate from public employee organizations, the administration of the merit system is greatly furthered by strong groups of public employees who work in its behalf. In some jurisdictions these are independent civil service associations, created primarily for social and beneficial services to their members which do not advocate collective bargaining, and in other jurisdictions they are trade unions.

The independent civil service associations have achieved their greatest strength and importance in California and Maryland. In the former state the California State Employees' Association has grown in twenty years to embrace more than one hundred councils with a total membership of about 40,000. The program of this association is so comprehensive in scope and so intelligent in leadership that competing organizations are unlikely to make much progress. While the California association strives for the improvement of the conditions of work among state employees, it does not attempt irregular interference with the administration of the civil service system. At the same time, it has announced that it expects the State Personnel Board will perform faithfully the responsibilities confided to it by law. The relationship between the state officials and the public employee leaders in California is one of mutual confidence and respect.

In Maryland the Maryland Classified Employees' Association, comprising about 50 per cent of the permanent civil service employees of the state, has declared its objectives as a triple obligation—to the state, to the taxpaying public, and to the state employees. Article II, Section 1, of the by-laws of the association reads: "The objects of this association shall be (1) to promote greater efficiency in the various departments of the state government;

(2) to obtain the maximum employment service to the state at the minimum cost to the taxpayer; and (3) to advise its members on any of their state employment problems, to protect their rights under the merit system, and generally to advance their economic and social welfare as state employees." The Maryland civil service system through the years has had the benefit of advice and support from the National Civil Service League. In other words, civil service reformers, state officials, and state employees have cooperated to ensure the success of public personnel administration in Maryland.

The weakness of independent civil service associations lies in the ease with which their leaders often succumb to the temptation to do the bidding of politicians to whom they give their first allegiance. These associations are no better than their leaders, who rise to their positions through political activity within the association. There is no supervision either of personnel or policies such as exists within the hierarchy of trade unionism. It is therefore frequently not difficult for the politicians to make deals with employee leaders who are willing for their own advantage to betray the membership of the association.

Some independent civil service associations have fallen into the error of participating actively in partisan politics. This is a fundamental mistake. Trying to influence elections is a game in which the civil service employees cannot win. The political parties, which operate on a state and national basis, will not overlook defeats administered to their candidates but will always take credit to themselves for victories. Public employee associations are therefore likely to receive no thanks for victories they may help to achieve and will be soundly condemned for defeats they may have helped to administer. Public employees, like all other citizens, should undertake their partisan political activities through the party organizations.

There is another and more practical reason why public employee groups should refrain from partisan political activities. When these groups urge their legitimate proposals for higher salaries, more generous pensions, shorter hours, and better working conditions, they must present their claims to legislators, freeholders, councilmen, and city commissioners who have gained their offices through hard-fought struggles by their party organizations. These elective officials are unlikely to look with favor upon proposals made by men whose hands are stained with the blood of party colleagues whom they have axed in the last election.

There are legitimate ends to be sought by civil service associations and similar public employee groups and by political party organizations. The former exist to better the condition of civil service employees, and the party organizations seek to fill the elective offices of government with persons of their choice. There can be no valid reason why a civil service employee should not belong to a public employee association and also to a political party. The tragic error in judgment comes when public employee associations attempt to take over the functions which belong to the party organization.

It is possible that civil service employee leaders will voluntarily refrain from political activity, but this is unlikely. The federal government was obliged to enact the Hatch Act in 1939 which prohibits any administrative employee of the United States from participating in partisan political activity. The prohibition is quite comprehensive and extends to those employees of state and local governments who are paid in whole or in part from federal funds. The statute is admittedly difficult of administration, but it has been enforced. The time is probably not far distant when state legislatures will find it necessary to come to the further support of their merit system laws by the enactment of "little Hatch Acts" designed to restrain all state and local civil service employees from participating in partisan political activities.

There is a real danger that these restrictive measures will hinder the development among civil service employees of vital and creative citizenship. It is highly desirable that public employees be encouraged to stand for elective offices. Knowledge gained in public employment can be utilized to advantage in improving the work of legislation and administration. Leaves of absence to civil service employees to campaign for election can be justified in the interest of better government. This encouragement of public employees to conduct themselves as citizens should not be perverted to permit the leaders of employee associations to throw their weight around in political campaigns. In the first place, these men almost never have any mandate from the rank and file of their membership to commit the association to particular candidates. The members of an association are divided among the parties and will vote as they please. In the second place, a commitment by employee leaders is nearly always based upon promises the redemption of which will not benefit the members of the association. They are agreements made among selfish men to advance their own interests. A clear distinction is required in the law between the legitimate concerns of the civil service employee as a citizen and the selfish interests of his association leaders. Legislative enactments thus far passed or proposed have not made this distinction.

The unions, which have been most successful among the employees of the federal government, have not become involved in partisan politics. That is not to say they have always refrained from taking sides in a campaign. Before the passage of the Hatch Act, there were several instances in which unions of federal employees supported candidates who had favored their measures in Congress and opposed other candidates who had shown hostility to union aims. However, it is important to note that these excursions into partisan politics were undertaken to defend the legitimate interests of the civil service employees. They did not extend to the advancement of causes of general concern. Since the Hatch Act became law there has been a scrupulous avoidance of partisan activity by civil service unions among the federal employees. Only one union of these employees has shown any indication of its interest in partisan conflicts. In state and local governments there has been an almost total disregard for partisan political activity by the unions.

At state and local government levels the best unions are to be found in Wisconsin and Minnesota. In these states the unions compare favorably with the independent civil service associations in California and Maryland. The Wisconsin state employees have formed local unions affiliated with the American Federation of State, County, and Municipal Employees (AFL). With intelligent leadership the union program in Wisconsin affords many opportunities for civil service employees to protect their own interests at the same time that they promote the welfare of the state. These unions have actively assisted in the recruitment of personnel for the state institutions and have urged their members to remain in the service of the state. The Minnesota unions, also affiliated with the American Federation of Labor, have not had as smooth sailing in recent years as the Wisconsin unions but they have been no less intelligent and courageous in their declarations of purpose. When the Minnesota salary-increase program sponsored by the trade unions was before the legislature in 1949, the word was passed to the union leaders that they would be likely to succeed if the state employees would agree to support in the next election "a certain member of the House." To this the union leaders replied: "If we cannot get an increase in salary above the board and through our work for the state, there is no reason for accepting the increases." The unions in Wisconsin and Minnesota and the independent associations in California and Maryland issue publications for the information of their members that might well become models for public employee organizations throughout the United States. Elsewhere the publications of state and local employee groups are too often devoted almost exclusively to voicing demands for higher salaries, abusing the appointing authorities and whining because the public does not display the high regard for government employees which they believe is due them.

The best administration of the civil service system will be found in those jurisdictions in which the best employee organizations exist. Whether these take the form of unions as in Wisconsin and Minnesota or independent civil service associations as in Maryland and California, the merit system benefits from support and criticism by alert employee groups. Further steps are required to enable good employee organizations, whatever may be their form, to play a more important role in solving the problem of employer-employee relationships.

The National Civil Service League in 1946 in its report on *Employee Organizations in the Public Service* declared: "Government should provide adequate machinery for cooperation, to remove causes of grievances, and promote the solution of problems and development of morale in the service. Officials should establish within their departments and agencies divisions of personnel management to operate such machinery in collaboration with employee representatives." This concise statement embraces two fundamental requirements for success in handling the issues which arise between the officers and employees of government. In the first place, the machinery must function in time to remove the *causes* of grievances. In the second place, it must be operated in collaboration with representatives of the employees. It is perhaps superfluous to add that the representatives must be selected by some method that will ensure a free choice.

If the machinery operates with timeliness and in response to direction from employees as well as officials, it will do more than forestall grievances. Collaboration means working together or jointly to achieve a common purpose. When the interested parties apply themselves in this way to the issues which confront them there will result constructive thinking calculated to effect lasting solutions.

The trade unions are unlikely to succeed in introducing the paraphernalia of collective bargaining into civil service jurisdictions. The success which has been achieved in the Tennessee Valley Authority and with the Bonneville Power Administration represents a limited use of collective-bargaining agreements in federal agencies which are unique in character. There is no basis for the belief that these experiments can be projected into broader fields of governmental activity. Indeed, there is no assurance that they would, at TVA or at Bonneville, survive a change of party in the government at Washington. It is most unlikely that public officials in state and local governments will abide by collective-bargaining agreements unless legal compulsion can be applied. The procedures for the solution of the problem of employer-employee relationships must be set up in the law.

The independent employee associations have been no more successful than the trade unions in appealing to civil service commissions where the issues extend beyond the narrow confines of the civil service law. The problem of employer-employee relationships is too broad to be brought within the jurisdiction of civil service agencies. Position classification, the recruitment and placement of personnel through sound testing procedures, the construction of good compensation plans, and the creation of merit rating programs are the tasks for the performance of which the central personnel agency has been staffed. When, in addition to these technical services a civil service commission is directed to hold hearings in cases of employees demoted, suspended, or dismissed from their positions, there comes into existence almost the whole of a civil service program. The technical services have generally been well done but experience has shown that at all levels of government there is need for supplementary agencies to undertake the other tasks of personnel administration.

Neither the unions nor the independent civil service associations can escape the charge that sometimes they encourage the exploitation of grievances for their own selfish purposes. Employee organizations are regularly competing for members among the permanent civil service employees. They seek to build a record of grievances redressed through the activities of their leaders with which to impress the rank and file of the employees and increase organization membership. Every civil service administrator is obliged to distinguish between bona fide grievances and "organization grievances" hatched by organization leaders to stimulate membership recruitment. Promises of higher salaries and better job classifications made to individual employees as inducements to join the organization will soon be followed by requests for hearings on charges of discrimination. In this way issues will be created which neither the employee nor the department head expected to arise. This sordid business will doubtless continue to plague public officials and civil service administrators until sound administrative controls of public personnel are established.

The problems of individual employees should be isolated from the larger problem of employer-employee relationships. It is true that the two are interrelated, but not to the extent they are made to appear by the public employees and their spokesmen. The most frequent individual grievance alleged arises out of dissatisfaction with compensation. It may be that the entire salary and wage scale of a jurisdiction is unreasonably low or it may be merely that an unsatisfactory employee is attempting to gain for himself advantages which he does not deserve. The problem of securing a sound compensation plan should not be confused with that of dealing with an employee who is complaining about his salary.

There will be incumbents of almost every class of positions who should not be advanced beyond the minimum salary of the positions for which they qualified. It is an injury to the intelligent and capable employees as well as the civil service system to grant increases regardless of merit to everybody within a class. Regular increments intended to reward the meritorious should not come to be considered rightly due the unfit. Efficiency ratings can be used as a basis for determining the desirability of periodic salary increases where rating plans are skillfully devised and competently administered. But the question whether an employee should receive periodic increases within his class title is one which must be determined by the department head upon the advice of the employee's supervisor. No employee ought to receive such increase, except upon recommendation of his supervisor. The worth of the service of any employee can be accurately determined only within the department where he is employed. The establishment of good personnel offices within the operating departments of government is not less important for the handling of the problems of individual employees than the creation of adequate machinery for the solution of the larger problem of employer-employee relationships.

There can be no final solution to the problem of employer-employee relationships in public employment. The issues which arise must be met candidly and courageously by public officials as well as public employees. They require cooperative efforts and constructive thinking on the part of the best minds among the officers and employees of government. At the present time some business agents of the unions, a very small number of independent civil service association leaders and a few enlightened public officials appear to grasp the significance of the problem of employer-employee relationships. Before greater progress can be made generally throughout the country toward creating a genuine partnership between the officers and employees of government it will be necessary to recruit for the public service more first-rate men and women. In this task of recruitment the educational system of the United States must undertake to play a distinctive part. When teachers in the schools, colleges, and universities are willing to prepare and direct their best students toward careers in the public service, improvements in the whole process of government can be expected.

CHAPTER IV

EDUCATION AND THE PUBLIC SERVICE

THE growth of public employment in the United States has presented a challenge to education that is immediate and direct. The schools and colleges are asked at once to train young men and women in the special skills required for government positions and to educate for citizenship in a self-governing commonwealth. This is an imposing task. Education is expected to provide what is in reality a vocational training under conditions which will instill in the students a devotion to the high ideals of a free government. In other words, there must be created a civil service which is not only competent to carry on the activities of government but also to reflect the principles inherent in American political institutions.

Training for salaried positions in the civil service must necessarily engage the attention of a system of education which aims to make its citizens self-supporting. But it would be dangerous for American education to concentrate too closely upon vocational training for public employment. It is neither possible nor desirable for schools, colleges, and universities to provide training for specific jobs in the government service. The jobs may not be available at any level of government when the training program has been completed. If there are no jobs, disillusionment and unhappiness will await the student who has confined his education to a narrow vocational preparation for a single governmental job. Fortunately few people are likely to make this mistake.

The bulk of vocational training programs aim to impart professional, technical, or scientific knowledge that is required by positions in private enterprise as well as public service. The student thinks of himself as studying for a particular profession and tends to identify himself with other members of the profession. He undertakes to equip himself with such professional knowledge that he can pass at will between a post in government and its counterpart in private enterprise. There is no need for the school or university to vary the training program in order to ensure professional competence on the part of its graduates in either public or private employment. The same fundamental qualifications are necessary in either case.

The schools of engineering, law, and business administration have prepared large numbers of men and women now in public employment. Others have graduated from schools of medicine, agriculture, public health, and veterinary science. An increasing number of public employees have studied in graduate schools in the liberal arts and in education. Some have consciously guided on the government service while pursuing their formal education, but more have thought only of the professional field they were at the time seeking to master.

The professional schools have their own traditional curricula upon which they place great emphasis. The strictly technical subjects are so numerous that they claim the entire attention of the student from the time of entrance to graduation. There is little opportunity in most professional schools for any acquaintance with the humanities or social studies. This must be obtained elsewhere.

The law schools have done much to improve the prelegal education of their students and something to elevate their own training programs. Since the advent of Dean Langdell and of the case method of studying law, the law schools of the country have provided the most precise and scientific training at the graduate level. They have surpassed the schools of business administration in the quality of their instruction and are far in advance of the training programs for public administration that have recently been undertaken in colleges and universities. But the law schools, if they are to succeed with their students, must ensure that these young men and women have learned the arts of self-expression before they embark upon their law studies.

It is precisely in this need for self-expression that the requirements of public employment are more rigorous than the demands of private enterprise. The importance of clarity in written communications is much greater in government than in business. The businessman requires a written record for immediate or impending transactions. The record is seldom detailed and not infrequently is confined in its scope to relatively simple matters. In government the normal means of communication is through written memoranda. A large number of public employees, some of them at great distance from the center of government, must be directed in the details of their work through the written word. Nothing is more certain to cause trouble than the badly turned phrase or the ambiguous sentence of an administrative order or directive. A politician in one of Disraeli's novels remarked: "Few ideas are correct ones, but with words we govern men." Since the written or spoken word is of the highest importance in government, the public employee must have a thorough command of language. Finally, the written record in government may be required in an investigation, often at a date remote from that of the events which are chronicled in the record. Congressional and other legislative investigations generally delve deeply into the files of administrative departments. The records therein contained must be clear and unmistakable as to their meaning.

Written and oral composition will not only clarify thought but also present the permanent record required in government. Career men and women often appear to be wasting valuable time as they strive to create memoranda which state precisely the desired objective. Of course, government employees as well as other people waste time, but painstaking application to composition brings rich rewards. The man or woman in search of a career in public employment cannot afford to neglect the constant improvement of the means of self-expression.

Much of the data embodied in public reports and government documents will be contained in graphs, charts, and lists of figures. Comprehension of these requires a knowledge of accounting and statistics. The man who prepares the statistical material requires a thorough understanding of the techniques of statistical science. It is also his obligation to present the finished product in such form that it can be readily assimilated by those to whom it is directed. This requires at least an elementary knowledge of statistical methods by all public employees who aspire to go forward in the service of government. Without this general acquaintance with statistics and accounting, much of the subject matter of government records will have little meaning to the very people for whose information it was prepared.

The value of statistical data in public administration has increased in recent years because the findings of particular public services have been made available to higher levels of administration. The public health service has long made use of morbidity tables, while the welfare administrators have made use of figures involving age, sex, and economic status of the population. However valuable such information may have been to the workers

in health and welfare, it was of little help to the administrator whose task was the coordination of all the services of government. It is an easy matter to apply the
statistical method in the collection of data in any social
science. But "as every serious student of social matters
knows by his own experience, it is impossible to touch
a physical fact, or a statistical datum, or a legal enactment, in reference to its social bearing, without its at
once, so to speak, coming alive in his hands, and attach-
ing itself to an underlying relation of mind as the only
unity which will make it intelligible, and correlate it
with other experiences, by themselves no less frag-
mentary." In order to escape the futility of regarding
mere dumb facts, important use must be made of the
statistical data assembled. This can be done only by men
and women who have been trained to understand the procedures through which the information was assembled.

In-service training is required at every level of government and there is no government agency which does
not have to provide some training for its employees after
they have been appointed. All that a civil service examination can do is to select those persons who are trainable
for the specific tasks to be performed in the positions
for which the tests have been advertised. It is idle to
suppose that a candidate for patrolman or fireman can
know about police and fire services in advance of any
practical experience. What a civil service department
or a personnel agency can do is to recruit the most likely
candidates for these services. Of course, there will always be appointing authorities who expect the central
personnel agency to certify eligibles fully prepared to
do all the tasks set forth in the job specification on the
public notice of the test. This unreasonable attitude has
led to many unfair criticisms of the civil service system.
Such criticisms reflect unfavorably not upon the system

whereby public employees are recruited but rather upon the intelligence of the appointing authorities.

Since all public agencies must provide some on-the-job training for their employees, it is important that training programs be carefully planned and executed. They must be proportioned to the nature and complexity of the work. A few months may be all that is required to obtain the maximum results from an intelligent clerk while a much longer period will be necessary to enable a college graduate to undertake difficult and complex assignments. No general statement can be made either about the kind or amount of in-service training required. These are matters to be determined by each agency.

More careful planning will result in greater competence among supervisory personnel and greater foresight in anticipating future needs in a government agency. The job specifications for most supervisory positions include the requirement that the incumbent shall train subordinates. This requirement is too often overlooked in making promotions. Men who possess particular skills are not always able to impart their knowledge to others. They fail as supervisors because they are not good teachers, although they may be highly skilled in the tasks to be performed.

A more frequent cause of human wastage in the public service springs from failure to anticipate future needs of an agency. If a service has been well planned, the specialized needs which arise can usually be foreseen. Personnel already on the payroll can be trained to take over the new duties, and replacements can be made at the entrance level. A department head who is caught without qualified personnel when he is directed by law to perform a service is easy prey for the politicians. Party chairmen and others take exuberant delight in coming to the rescue of the department head by suggesting just the right man for the job. When an appointment has been made under these conditions, political pressures to secure permanent tenure for what in reality is a patronage choice become insistent.

It is always difficult to explain why nobody within the agency was ready to pick up new duties when these have been directed to be performed. Of course, the permanent employees of the department are fully aware of the situation. They try to teach their new masters the tasks which they could have performed more efficiently and more economically if they had only been afforded the opportunity. Meanwhile, the department head has lost the confidence and respect of his subordinates. He fails as the political head when he shirks his first obligation as an administrator, which is to train his employees to undertake the duties entrusted to him. As a public official he has failed to perform the duties of his office faithfully, impartially, and justly to the best of his ability. He should be removed.

The academic study of public administration will do something by way of training for public employment, although it is doubtful whether we shall in this country establish an administrative class whose members can be recruited and trained on the basis of a general education in administration. The American practice of testing for the job promises to be the method we shall follow in recruitment. Furthermore, public opinion does not support the idea of a class of administrators who have not learned their skills through grappling with the concrete problems of the public service. The student of public administration must therefore regard his subject as a cultural discipline rather than a vocational training.

Public administration at present may appear to some critics to be a dull subject because it has led to the construction of no convincing theory of administration. It has little of the appeal to the imagination possessed by political theory or public law. But if it appears dull it is with a significant dullness. Public administration has already exorcised many dogmatic assumptions about the operations of government based upon an environment which has already passed away. Intelligent teachers recognize that "public administration is not a bounded area but a center of interest and effort." It flourishes in proportion to its ability to effect substantial contacts with other fields of human knowledge only to see its ideas appropriated by the more conventional disciplines and made a part of the common stock of human thought. "In public administration the scholars and the teachers have no choice but to continue in the uncomfortable role of frontiersmen."

There is sound reason for the public employee to keep abreast of the developments in the academic study of public administration. By no other means can he become more certainly aware of the emerging relationships which are so important in the formulation of public policy. The structure of government and the constitutional limitations under which government must operate have long been subjects of study in schools, colleges, and universities. What men have thought about the nature of the state and of political institutions goes back to the time of Plato and Aristotle. But the student of public administration cannot avoid dealing with leadership at top levels in government. The relations between the executive and the legislature, the effect of the stimuli from strong executive leadership and the reaction to adverse decisions in legislative bodies engage the attention of students of public administration almost exclusively. They cannot be expected to tell in advance what ought to be done, and teachers of character among them would not lay claim to such political wisdom. But academic studies in public administration can explore the many problems which arise out of the relationships which must of necessity be formed among the participants in the governmental process. Wise public employees will be alert to the discoveries in public administration.

The chief danger which threatens academic studies of public administration is that teachers and scholars will be pressed to claim too much in behalf of their subject. Public administration cannot teach anybody to administer anything regardless of the thing to be administered. It is not a training program for a new vocation but a means of reaching a better understanding of the functioning of governmental institutions that are very old. The teacher of public administration already has two strikes against him when he embarks upon his task. He is certain to be regarded as a long-haired theoretician and he will surely be charged with never having met a payroll. He is therefore viewed askance from the outset by politicians and men of business. The only way a teacher of public administration can secure for himself and his work the respect of other people is through the cultivation of judgment.

What is presently attempted by the academic study of public administration is important not only to public employees but also to every citizen. Within the range of its concern, a course on public administration embraces all the social sciences. The catholicity of its approach enables public administration to implant in its students a high degree of understanding of all the processes of government. "The best laws," said Aristotle, "will be of no avail unless the young are trained by habit and education in the spirit of the constitution." A broad political education is required for a people who are to govern themselves.

Education and the Public Service

Education in the United States should assume that every citizen will participate in public affairs. Of course, everybody will not enter the civil service or seek public office. Some may never do more than vote or perform jury duty. But the educational system should inspire young men and women to take an active interest in their government. No citizen can refrain from making intelligent decisions in public affairs without loss to the country and to himself. The warning of Jean Jacques Rousseau should not be forgotten: "As soon as any man says of the affairs of the state, *what does it matter to me?* the state is lost."

The efforts of schools, colleges, and universities to provide an education which will enable their graduates to earn a living at the same time that they play a role in public affairs have not been wholly successful. A recent report of the Citizenship Clearing House states: "There is too little being done by American colleges and universities in preparing young men and women for actual participation in politics; in other words, in operating our democratic system of government. Of their failure in this respect college and university authorities are only vaguely conscious. Modern trends in education, including the vast development in recent years of the social sciences, have not materially bettered the situation and in some respects have made it worse."

This pessimistic report was based largely upon a survey of the introductory course in political science in more than two hundred American colleges and universities. The chief criticism of the content of the introductory course was the uniformity of its pattern and the want of originality in the methods of its teaching. Neither in content nor in methods were most introductory courses calculated "to prepare students for and motivate them towards active participation in politics."

If the content and methods of political science courses in our own day are unattractive, the professors fall far short of the ideal attained in earlier days. The number of teachers in the introductory courses who have had substantial political experience is small. This is not wholly the fault of the teachers, because college presidents and trustees do not always look with favor upon active participation in public affairs of faculty members. The result has been that most professors have not had the kind of political experience that would teach them much of the art of politics.

The survey disclosed that only 16.3 per cent of the 477 professors concerning whose qualifications information was available had held elective offices or undertaken party services in the sense of membership on party committees, attendance at party conventions, participation in campaigns, and candidacy for office. A few professors had been appointed to honorary positions on boards and other unsalaried positions where the political experience was not significant. Others were listed as consultants, but consulting positions are proof of professional competence and not of political experience. "The largest class of positions—the administrative—was made up for the most part of routine jobs largely in the classified service. Such positions on any level of government have very little to do with politics. . . . This is especially true, however, in the federal service where the bulk of the positions listed are buried deep in the official hierarchy. Nearly half of the jobs held, omitting elective offices, were federal jobs of this character."

It might be argued that this survey of a single course in political science in a few institutions is insufficient basis for an indictment if the professors themselves did not agree in the main with the conclusions. A committee of the American Political Science Association in 1941 reported: "It may be questioned whether political scientists are sufficiently in touch with the phenomena which they study and teach. Too often they study government only through the use of books and the printed word, and thus cannot bring to their research or teaching the lively sense of reality and the grasp of the important issues which come only through first-hand contacts."

These strictures are not essentially different from those contained in a committee report to the same association in 1914, where it was charged that political science courses were too theoretical and recommended that greater attention be given to the actual working of political institutions. One professor remarked: "The teacher has long been told that his main function was to 'set the pupil's heart right.' It is his equal function to 'set the student's facts right.' Now the only person at all qualified to teach the actual facts as to government, it seems to me, is the one who has been, himself, a part of the creative forces that make government. He who reads from the textbook and repeats what is in the textbook without having lived through what the processes of government really mean will never make a teacher worthy of the student, be the student in the grades, in the high school or in the university.

"The fundamental business of the teacher of political science is to train for citizenship, and no one is trained for citizenship who does not have his mind taken from the formal things in government to the actual things. This can be done only by the teacher who is himself a factor in government processes."

It must be admitted that many teachers of political science have long been aware of the need to vivify the classroom instruction through participation in the processes of government. The difficulty has been to get professors appropriately placed in the governmental system where they could make some important contribution at the same time that they learned more about government. There is no doubt that the appointment of a professor to an important position in the government of state or nation will arouse opposition among the professional politicians. These men fear the entry into public life of anybody who cannot be controlled by the normal methods of party discipline.

Sometimes attempts have been made to bring into college and university faculties men who have served in important public offices and convert them into scholars. "Candidates for conversion," it has been pointed out, "are not scarce and the policy is tempting. It can be done, but it is difficult. Adjustment to academia for the convert is fully as difficult as adjustment to public life for the academician, although the man of affairs does not suspect it when he dons academic robes. A young man sufficiently flexible and humble to make the transition easily lacks the standing and experience to make him an attractive importation. Consequently, students and colleagues suffer, not always in silence, until the man of affairs masters the scholar's role." This is seldom done successfully. What more often happens is that the man of affairs returns to public life when he finds how hard a teacher must work to improve his teaching and research. An academic post is not a soft featherbed upon which a public official may flop when his party is out of power.

A full-time faculty in political science can be supplemented by the employment of public officials on a part-time basis or as special lecturers. In this way special professional services which would otherwise be lacking may be brought to a college or university campus. But the proper utilization of these special services requires on the part of the full-time professors an understanding of the whole process of government of which the nonacademic teachers are merely a segment. If special or part-time teachers are hired only because the members of the faculty on regular appointment are unable to find the time to develop and present the subject matter, the special employments can be justified. But it would be difficult to suppose that young men and women would be motivated toward careers in public affairs by temporary and casual contacts of this kind.

A college or university faculty is a company of scholars whose lives are dedicated to the instruction of youth. The professors have different professional interests because they teach a variety of subjects, but all of them have a common interest in the advancement of human knowledge and in imparting to their students what share of this knowledge they possess. The spiritual and cultural life of an educational institution depends upon the influence which its faculty can exercise over the students. It is unlikely that a young man will become interested in public affairs unless he has sensed in his college or university the existence of a common interest in scholarship which transcends the selfish interests of individuals.

The teacher of political science must find his own way into public affairs at levels which will enable him to serve the government at the same time that he enriches his own scholarship. This may mean that he will from time to time leave the campus briefly to hold public office. Elsewhere it may require regular but only part-time contacts with public officials in the professor's study or at the seat of government. Whatever may be the approach of the professor of political science to the realities of public service, it must involve matters of sufficient importance to justify enlisting the attention of a trained and mature mind. But no professor can afford to become so preoccupied with the duties of a public post that he neglects his obligation to his institution and his colleagues to contribute to the company of scholars.

It is perhaps superfluous to remark that the study of political science is not the only avenue to active participation in politics. Plenty of people have gone to high positions in government without having taken a course or read a textbook in political science. But political science today purports to deal with the theory and practice of government. It is the only subject in the curriculum of high schools, colleges, and universities which deals exclusively with the phenomena of politics. The students therefore have a right to expect that teachers of political science will give them the most precise and effective guidance when they turn in the direction of public careers. This guidance the teachers can provide only if they have qualified themselves by training and experience for the task.

The question may well be raised whether the large number of courses in political science offered in our institutions of higher learning does not tend to discourage young men and women from embarking upon public careers. The training required for participation in public affairs is broader than that designed to promote commercial or industrial efficiency. Too much emphasis in schools and colleges upon political science may restrict unduly the intellectual horizon of the prospective candidate for elective or appointive office and even for the civil service. Aristotle saw the problem of training for the public service correctly when he advocated the education of all citizens in the spirit of the constitution. By that he meant that everyone should be disciplined toward an ethical center in which service to the state is paramount. The Greek ideal of public service therefore placed character as the most important requirement for participation in public affairs.

Education and the Public Service

There have been from time to time other tests of fitness for public service. Machiavelli in the sixteenth century lauded efficiency as he declared material prosperity to be the end of the state. France before 1789 clung to the idea that only the weightier part of the population should concern itself with government. Public affairs belonged to the aristocracy. At the formation of the American political system, the rich, the well-born, and the educated were thought to be the only citizens whose political aspirations deserved gratification. Politics was exclusively the business of gentlemen. With the advance of popular education and the broadening of the franchise, aristocratic pretensions have almost wholly disappeared, and the phrases of Lincoln in his immortal Gettysburg Address have set the pattern for the United States.

Character has remained the enduring test of fitness for public office or public employment. If a man lacks integrity, he will also lack the virtue and wisdom which are essential to popular government. The loyalty oaths which are springing up in statutes and executive orders in state and nation are clumsy attempts to ensure character in the elected officials and in the civil service. Such tests of loyalty may be necessary, but their very existence is somehow evidence that we have failed to provide the broad ethical foundation which is requisite to success in free government.

The older education in the United States boldly asserted that it was a training for wisdom and character. Since it was based on the belief that men need to be disciplined to some ethical center, it taught the conquest of self, which is the first requisite of leadership. The closely prescribed courses of study in schools and colleges were not intended to permit wide variations among individuals. Everybody followed pretty much the same program. The trouble was that not enough boys and girls followed the program to its conclusion. When compulsory education laws were introduced, the school system had to take into account the differences among pupils and modify the curricula accordingly.

Until recently education in the United States was firmly seated in the humanities. Classics and mathematics formed the core of studies in our schools and colleges. More recently Latin and Greek have grudgingly given place to modern languages, and history has become respectable in the training of the mind. But down to World War II humanistic studies, although somewhat altered in aspect and at times shaken in purpose, held their own in competition with social studies and the natural sciences. The arts and literature, with some assistance from the historians, continued to attract a majority of our young men and women in search of a liberal education.

Following the cessation of hostilities, the humanities suffered sharp reductions in enrollments because returning veterans were interested to obtain immediate financial rewards from their delayed education. The men came back from war service to crowd the courses in history, economics and political science while philosophy, religion, and the fine arts were momentarily neglected in the belief that other subjects contributed more directly to the increase of acquisitive capacity. The flight from the humanities proved to be temporary and can be attributed to the war. Within a brief period the vitality of humanistic studies was once again revealed as young men and women flocked to courses in the arts and literature. If there had been no war, and the young men had continued to come directly to college from the secondary schools, the humanities would doubtless have enjoyed an uninterrupted prosperity.

Modern education cannot afford to permit the humanities to be displaced in the programs of individual students. They are important to an understanding of mankind. Without their help other studies lack direction and purpose. The needs of society require that the arts, philosophy, and literature establish a balance with social studies and the natural sciences. The explanation for the rise of the social sciences is that they alone are competent to enable the present generation of students to solve the problems of the modern world. This appears somewhat specious in the light of what has already taken place within different branches of the social sciences. Man is always trying to simplify his environment by pointing to a single cause for an effect which is in reality complex. The propensity of the human mind to attempt simple solutions in complex situations has had a marked and not too healthy effect upon the social sciences. Political science has undergone some of the deterioration that has infected all social studies.

Political science traces its lineage to the works of Plato and Aristotle, who wrote commentaries on the passing scene. To be sure, it was somewhat sour commentary. Both writers deplored the decline of the Greek city-state and viewed with alarm the rise of imperialism under Philip of Macedon. But Plato and Aristotle gave to political science an abiding sense of reality as they sought to describe the principles which man must follow if he is to control his political destiny. What has happened to political science is not that its fundamental principles have been obscured but that these have been perverted by the zeal of reformers.

The history of political theory has been called the history of propaganda. Movements of reform and even of revolution have not disdained the guidance of political science. The result has been that political science has frequently lost touch with reality as it has become embroiled in political controversy. When the dust of conflict has settled, a pattern of thought emerges in which principles have been sacrificed to expediency. Students are frequently confronted with the accomplishments of a political upheaval in which they are led to believe that substantial progress has been made toward the attainment of truth and justice. In reality all that has occurred is the displacement of one set of forces by another, without in any way touching the fundamental principles of human behavior. Somebody has gained and somebody has lost in every far-reaching political controversy, but political science has been weakened every time it has given its aid to the combatants.

Those who aspire to careers in the public service would do well to partake sparingly of the social sciences and then only in combination with other disciplines. One should not be deceived by the labels placed upon the goods displayed on academic shelves. A thorough understanding of Plato and Aristotle may prove to be of greater practical value than a roster of courses on contemporary topics. The education which succeeds is that which trains for wisdom and character. These are the qualities of the mind and the spirit which are needed not only in public service but also in every walk of life. They can be obtained in a variety of ways.

Education at the college level for active participation in public affairs began on this side of the Atlantic in colonial days. The arrival of President Witherspoon in Princeton during the summer of 1768 was also the occasion of an announcement that the College of New Jersey would provide training "to fit young Gentlemen for serving their Country in public Stations."* There was nothing remarkable about this statement of purpose. Political education was also one of the avowed objects at Yale and the College of Philadelphia. The importance of the Princeton announcement lies in the results which were subsequently achieved. For in the coming of the Scotch Presbyterian clergyman, the College of New Jersey was enabled to give to a paper program the substance of reality.

Higher education in the American colonies had originally been designed for the training of clergymen. With the single exception of the College of Philadelphia, founded by Benjamin Franklin, the colonial institutions of learning arose under religious leadership. Harvard, which was first authorized by a vote of the Massachusetts General Court in 1636, remained for many years the stronghold of Puritanism. The second American college was William and Mary in Virginia, chartered by the Crown in 1693 and launched under Anglican control. When Dr. James Blair, an Anglican of Scotch origin, first broached the subject of a collegiate charter to the attorney-general and urged that the people of Virginia had souls to be cared for, he was greeted by the explosion: "Damn their souls! Let them make tobacco." But the learned doctor was persistent and finally obtained the charter. A few years later, under the influence of the Mathers and other New England Puritans, Yale was chartered by the legislature of Connecticut to fit youths "for publick employment both in Church and Civil State."

Whatever may have been the intentions of the founders of Yale regarding the education of young men for

---

* An account of Dr. Witherspoon's program of education will be found in my article "Political Education in the Time of John Witherspoon," *Princeton Alumni Weekly*, XXVIII, pp. 487-490. February 10, 1928.

the public service, the course of study remained until almost the end of the eighteenth century a training for the ministry. Changes in the curriculum and in the methods of instruction were strenuously opposed on the ground that new ideas would undermine the influence of the New England clergy. The students who had heard of Locke, Descartes, and Newton, and desired an acquaintance with the newer ideas, were told that a new philosophy would bring in a new divinity and overthrow their cherished beliefs. Locke's *Essay concerning the Human Understanding* subsequently became a textbook at the New Haven college. But as an antidote to its liberal principles the students were required to read the compendium of Wollebius and Ames's *Medulla Theologicae*, two books which had long been in use in preparing nonconformist preachers.

Yale outwardly became the stronghold of orthodoxy. Noah Hobart prophesied that "the Old Religion of the Country, the Colonial Doctrines, as they are called, will be established in the House, there perpetually taught and rivetted in the minds of the Pupils, and they will go out into the world trammell'd with those trite doctrines of the Insufficiency of Human Reason." He was not far wrong. Freedom of thought was wholly suppressed. President Stiles states that he undertook to conduct recitations upon Jonathan Edwards' *Inquiry on the Will*, but "this giving offense was dropped." It was not until after the war for independence that the narrow curriculum was exploded by contact with the newer currents of thought in philosophy and education.

In marked contrast to the New England colleges, the College of New Jersey was established without mention of any set purpose to educate for the ministry. Although the college was nominally under Presbyterian control, the charter of 1748, which supplanted the earlier instrument, provided "that those of every religious denomination may have free and equal liberty and advantages of education . . . , and different sentiments in religion notwithstanding." The one avowed purpose of the college was to enable the youth of the provinces to be "instructed in the Learned Languages and in the Liberal Arts and Sciences." The college was devised neither as a church nor a state institution, and the trustees and faculty were unhampered by any of the restrictions which limited academic freedom in New England and Virginia.

With the situation at Princeton wholly favorable to his project, Dr. Witherspoon canvassed for students to return after graduation to pursue advanced studies designed to prepare them for public careers. He was fortunate in his first graduate students. James Madison, with his classmate Hugh Henry Brackenridge, returned in 1771 to be followed a year later by William Bradford. A beginning was thus made in graduate instruction. But the formal lectures originally intended to be given only to graduates were soon offered to juniors and seniors. The reason was probably the lack of funds for the maintenance of separate graduate courses. However, the result was to introduce into the undergraduate curriculum the scheme of political education.

The declared purpose of President Witherspoon was not only training for citizenship but also the production of statesmen. This was an ambitious program. But Dr. Witherspoon recognized that political education does not consist wholly or even largely in mere acquisitive scholarship. He was too conscious of his own intellectual growth under the stimulus of a varied and active public career to believe that textbooks or classroom lectures could furnish the complete equipment of the statesman. But he did believe that the college could train the mind and, by a careful adaptation of its courses, contribute directly to prepare its graduates for public careers.

Accounts of the lives of President Witherspoon's 478 graduates will be found in the biographical records of the college. One hundred and fourteen entered the ministry and a large number attained prominence in education. But most conspicuous of all the graduates were the men who entered public life. James Madison became President of the United States, and Aaron Burr served one term as Vice-President. Ten became cabinet officers. In the Continental Congress Dr. Witherspoon could count 6 of his graduates among his colleagues. Thirty-nine became representatives and 21 senators in the Congress of the United States; 12 were governors of states and 56 were chosen to state legislatures. Thirty became judges, 3 others being appointed to the Supreme Court of the United States. Of the 25 college graduates in the Federal Convention, 9 were Princetonians and 6 of these had President Witherspoon's signature on their diplomas.

It would be a mistake to refer the successful public careers of Dr. Witherspoon's graduates to the scheme of their formal education. For a course of liberal studies the president promised too much; for a training in the technique of public affairs he accomplished too little. The plan was fundamentally a protest against the desiccated course of study which marked the colonial college as a "clerical manufactory." But it had the end in view of encouraging the individual to develop his intellectual powers to the limits of his capacity. Without despising scholarship, Dr. Witherspoon repeatedly affirmed his belief that "in the middle regions of genius there are often those who reap the greatest benefit from education and study. . . . A very great genius is often like a very fine flower, to be wondered at, but of little service either for food or medicine." Nor was a youth to be abandoned as uneducable because he proved not to be proficient in every branch of knowledge. "A total want of capacity for one branch of science," the president remarked, "is not inconsistent even with a great capacity for another." The course of study was unique in eighteenth century colleges in that it attempted a selective process whereby students were directed toward those fields for which they showed the greatest aptitude. But the educational success of Dr. Witherspoon must be considered due in large measure to the personality of the man.

The curriculum of the eighteenth century college, although inadequate to the requirements of modern life, was founded upon the belief that students after graduation would play important roles in society. The course of study attempted to pass on the priceless heritage of the past with the injunction to advance still further the body of human knowledge. At Princeton, Yale, and the College of Philadelphia students were taught to look forward to careers of service to the country. Whether a man entered the ministry or sought a career in law, education, or public affairs, he was expected to devote his talents to the improvement of the social and political institutions under which he lived. College education was therefore directed toward training for the public service.

Throughout the development of American education from the elementary school to the university there has been a marked devotion to the fundamental worth of the individual. School systems have been devised to enable the pupil to make the most of his opportunities rather than to mould him to a pattern. Although boys and girls must remain in school at least until the years of adolescence, they have wide range of choice in the subjects which they are to study. There has never been any deviation in American education from the principles of the founding fathers that government exists for the benefit of the individual. The purpose of education has been to give the people insight into the institutions under which they live.

There is an intimate relationship between the system of education in a country and the forms of its government. "Governments, like clocks, go from the motion men give them," wrote William Penn in the preface to his *Frame of Government of Pensilvania*, "and as governments are made and moved by men, so by them they are ruined too. Wherefore governments rather depend upon men than men upon governments." Nearly three hundred years after the time of Penn, the people of the United States are becoming conscious of the fact that good government depends upon intelligent and trained personnel in all its branches. The training of such personnel is the task to which schools, colleges, and universities throughout the country must address themselves. Implicit in the accomplishment of the task is the assumption that the policies and practices of government and the educational institutions are interrelated.

CHAPTER V

ADMINISTRATIVE CONTROL OF PUBLIC PERSONNEL

THE ideal of maximum public services at minimum cost to the taxpayers can be achieved throughout the three great levels of government in the United States only through administrative control of public personnel. Reliance upon merit system laws will afford safeguards against the entry of unfit persons into public employment and will banish the grosser forms of personal and political patronage. The waste of public funds through payrolls swollen by the inclusion of unwanted positions and the maintenance of unnecessary services cannot be restrained by the merit system. The important unfinished business of civil service reform is to assist in providing the essential controls which will restrict public employment to the necessary requirements of government.

The management of public payrolls can result in enormous savings of public funds. Salaries and wages comprise the largest single item regularly recurring in public budgets. There are at least four ways in which economies can be effected in most governments through reductions in payrolls. First, sinecures can be abolished. The maintenance of unnecessary positions with which to reward party services is becoming increasingly difficult where adequate supervision of public expenditures is required. Second, the elimination of services which are no longer required should lead to reductions in force. Services no longer required should not be continued solely for the purpose of retaining employees on the payroll. Third, transfers of services from one level of government to another where they can be more economically performed should not be blocked by employee pressure groups seeking to prevent the abolition of jobs. The greatest single obstacle to consolidation and the readjustment of services among local governments is the pressure of employees and subordinate officials for job protection. Finally, very great savings in state and local jurisdictions could be made if the government would turn over to private enterprise many of the services now being uneconomically performed by public employees. Many governments are attempting to perform services which could be more cheaply and efficiently undertaken by private contractors if put out to competitive bidding. This is particularly true in municipal governments where large forces of semi-skilled and unskilled labor are employed by public authorities without adequate supervision. A change from public to private performance under government supervision of the scavenger services of a municipality might throw several hundred employees off the payroll but it would often result in large savings to the taxpayers. Whether changes affecting payrolls should be made are policy decisions which must be made by the officers of government.

Firm administrative control over the amount and quality of public personnel is necessarily placed in the hands of the chief executive. He is responsible to the electorate for the successful conduct of the government subject to appropriate supervision by the legislature. If he cannot at all times direct the activities of the public employees, he is unable to discharge his obligations to the people. The chief executive requires on the one hand protection against the insistent demands of his partisans that they be rewarded by appointments for services rendered to the party. The establishment of the merit system supplies this protection. On the other hand, he must be safeguarded against the pressures exerted by civil service employees not merely to retain their jobs but also to block any changes which will disturb them in their employment. This calls for generous powers of control and efficient machinery through which to exercise these powers. The aims of civil service reform are fulfilled only by the establishment of sound administrative control over public personnel.

Civil service reform in the United States was first considered in relation to the reduction in the costs of government. The Joint Select Committee on Retrenchment was created in July 1866 with the purpose "to discover useless offices and sinecures, extravagant salaries and allowances and other unnecessary and wasteful expenditures." The committee was revived by the Fortieth Congress in March 1867 and attention was directed by Mr. Jenckes of Rhode Island to the reform of the civil service as an effective means of reducing the costs of government. A sub-committee on civil service was created specifically instructed "to consider amendment of the law . . . to provide for the selection of subordinate officers after due examination . . . their continuance in office during specified terms . . . and for withdrawing the public services from being used as an instrument of political or party patronage." It was in pursuance of this legislative mandate that the famous Jenckes Report of 1868 was prepared, the ultimate aim of which was to introduce economy into the federal government through the reform of the civil service.

Mr. Jenckes and his associates obtained much data on the results of civil service reform in other countries. They also submitted a questionnaire to be answered by subordinate officers in the different departments of the federal government. These included the branch offices throughout the United States as well as the offices at Washington. A study of the questions asked indicates that the questionnaire was part of an economy survey. Heads of departments were asked not only whether they would be able through competitive tests to obtain better employees but also the extent to which they could probably reduce payrolls by the employment of more qualified people. The returns favored the introduction of competitive examinations at the same time that they promised definite reductions in the working force when better employees were forthcoming.

The reform of the civil service would perhaps have failed if it had been obliged to rest solely upon the economy it would introduce into the government. Members of Congress in the years following the death of Lincoln had other interests which bulked larger in their minds than reducing the costs of government. The majority were concerned with ways and means of perpetuating the Republican party, and all were involved to some extent in the struggles between President Johnson and Congress. The time had not yet arrived when executive power could be increased by giving the President greater control over the civil service.

It had become apparent to all that if civil service reform were to be undertaken it must be as a result of increased executive control. The proposals for reform which had preceded the Civil War involved two fundamental errors. The first was that they aimed to hinder removals rather than to control appointments. The second was that, by trying to shift power from the President to the Senate and associate that body in appointments, the responsibility was divided. Fortunately none of these proposals became law. When the Jenckes Report was presented there was no alternative except to increase the power of the President—or do nothing. Congress chose for the time to do nothing.

Meanwhile, the patronage squabbles continued to exhaust the President and to alarm the country. President Grant in his second annual message asked for a law which would "govern, not the tenure, but the manner of making all appointments." His attempts to control the distribution of the patronage under the act of March 3, 1871, were at the same time accompanied by a number of offensive appointments. Undoubtedly President Grant was desirous of securing a reform of the civil service but he recognized that he could do little without the active support of Congress. When he was succeeded by President Hayes, the movement for civil service reform had gained adherents throughout the country. The New York Civil Service Reform Association was formed in 1877 to be followed by societies in Boston, Philadelphia, Milwaukee, San Francisco, and other cities. These organizations in August 1881 helped to form the National Civil Service Reform League.

The agitation for reform outside government circles was based upon the widespread fear that democratic institutions were threatened by continued reliance upon patronage appointments. The Jenckes Report had asserted that "the partisan obligations of the candidate for office have been held to be of more consequence than his qualifications for the place for which he is a candidate, and every department of the government has been 'used as an instrument of political or party patronage.' . . ." Abundant evidence had been gathered from department heads to show "the evil effects of this custom of discharging well-trained officers, and of appointing unskilled persons in their places." To the demand for governmental economy was added a strong public sentiment in favor of elevating the whole moral tone of government by separating public employment from partisan politics. In the development of the general movement for reform, the changes which took place in the British civil service between 1855 and 1870 afforded much assistance.

The reform of the British civil service was undertaken neither in the interest of governmental economy nor for the protection of democratic institutions. It began in 1853 with the introduction of competitive tests in the Indian service, where greater efficiency was required for the employees than could be obtained through patronage appointments. At the same time, a report of a Treasury committee sponsored by Sir Stafford Northcote and Sir Charles Trevelyan proposed open competition for the home service. This report led to the Order in Council of 1855 which created a civil service commission and fixed minimum qualifications for appointments. Competitive tests were introduced five years later, and the Order in Council of 1870 instituted the rule of open competitive examinations as the normal mode of entry into the civil service.

The significance of the British reform in the civil service lay in the ability of the executive to bring about changes despite the hostility of Parliament. Of course, Parliament could have thwarted executive action, but this it did not choose to do. The parliamentary franchise had already undergone one change in 1832 and was to suffer a further enlargement in 1867. Parliamentary leaders were not disposed to assert partisan interests too eagerly. The time was opportune for the Crown to act in removing essential employees of government from the patronage. The news of what was taking place in England was regularly brought to the United States in correspondence among the leaders of the reform movement. Across the Atlantic the account of a 9½ per cent reduction in the total costs of salaries following the introduction of the British civil service system was not less impressive than the control by the executive of the distribution of the patronage upon a basis of merit and fitness. Civil service reform in England appeared to combine the efficiency of the German bureaucracy with democratic controls.

The German civil service system down to the revolution of 1918 was in many respects the ideal of efficiency in public administration. It originated after the close of the Thirty Years War to meet the requirements of Frederick William, Elector of Brandenburg, in his struggles against the feudal overlords and the urban holders of wealth. These special interests were uprooted by strengthening the executive organization to the point where the civil service became the real government of the realm.

The civil service reached its full flowering in the reign of Frederick the Great. By the end of his active career patronage had been completely superseded by appointments based upon merit. The merit principle was supplemented by insistence upon adequate theoretical education in those academic disciplines which were concerned with the state and its government. Frederick the Great required aspirants for the higher civil service positions to pass two, and in some cases three, examinations. Practical knowledge was not less important than academic attainments. Promotions depended upon sound craftsmanship exhibited at every stage of progress from entrance into the service. For more than two hundred years the German civil service proved to be incorruptible.

The German experience was less helpful to the American civil service reformers than the very much briefer record of accomplishment in Great Britain. While both

German and British universities came to play an important role in each country in the preparation of young men for the civil service, they differed in the purpose of their education. The inflexible formalism of the German training was not adapted to the American requirements. People in this country wanted education to produce merit and fitness, but they described these qualities in terms of character and self-reliance rather than as the result of specialized technical training. They did not want the civil service in the United States to become a bureaucracy. From the English experience, men like George William Curtis and Dorman B. Eaton believed they could derive the necessary lodgment of administrative control in the executive at the same time that they avoided the pitfalls of an undue reliance upon an administrative hierarchy. They emphasized the building of character as an integral part of education without neglecting the requirement of professional competence for admission to the civil service. In their judgment, the importance of the merit system was in its exclusion of the incompetent and unfit from entrance. "If we keep the front door carefully guarded," said Mr. Curtis, "the back door will take care of itself." In other words, civil service reform in its initial stages in the United States was satisfied to leave in the hands of administrative officials complete control of the public employees after these had been selected following open competition. Subsequently the view came to be accepted which was embodied in the Lloyd-LaFollette Act, that a dismissal from the civil service should be accompanied by reasons and that an opportunity should be given the employee to reply. The right of an employee to a public hearing on the reasons for his dismissal was not intended to permit his reinstatement over the objections of the officer who had removed him. All that was sought was the reconciliation of the merit system with the fundamental principles of democracy inherent in all American political institutions.

The American political system requires popular consent but it also demands efficient management. The elected officials can claim a direct mandate given at the last election for all their acts. What the people expect is that the elected officials will manage the government to the end that the greatest amount of public services will be provided with the least outlay of public funds. If mistakes are made, the elected officials will be retired to private life at the close of their terms. The public employees had their share in the processes of popular government when they entered the civil service system. At that time they were afforded equality of opportunity in accordance with merit and fitness. They were protected against personal and political patronage in obtaining their jobs. Thereafter the public employees became a part of the government subject to the direction and control of the political officials. Of course, the public employees have their legitimate interests in adequate salaries and decent working conditions, but these do not entitle them to intrude upon the framing or execution of the general policies of the government.

The federal government in recent years has twice undertaken the diagnosis of ailments which arise from inadequate personnel control. The President's Committee on Administrative Management in 1937 proposed to supplant the United States Civil Service Commission by a single executive officer, to be known as the Civil Service Administrator, and a nonsalaried Civil Service Board of seven members appointed by the President. The Civil Service Administrator would take over full direction and supervision of the civil service system and also act as the direct adviser to the President on all personnel matters and be responsible to him for the development of improved personnel policies and practices throughout the service. The Civil Service Board of seven lay advisers was expected not only to be the watchdog of the merit system but also to enlist the interest and cooperation of business, agriculture, labor, education, and the professions in improving the government service as a career. The proposed plan of organization was ridiculed in some government circles as Snow White and the Seven Dwarfs, and it was not adopted.

The failure of the proposals of the President's Committee on Administrative Management to secure congressional approval should not be construed as a denial of the need for more adequate control of public personnel. The evils in the existing situation were too obvious to be glossed over, and the need for remedial action was too pressing to be gainsaid. Where the committee erred was in the fundamental assumption that the President by a closer association with the technical features of the merit system could gain greater control over the administration of the entire public service. The report of the committee correctly states that personnel administration is the core of public administration. However, it fails to recognize that the whole of personnel administration is not comprised in the attainment of perfection in the merit system. The President was offered a technician as his personnel officer when what he requires is staff assistance which can direct his attention to the desirable readjustments in the public services necessary to carry out the policies to which his party is committed. The President does not have the time, and probably lacks the interest, to concern himself with improvements in the merit system. What he requires is competent personnel completely loyal to the policies dictated by the

President and Congress. He must recruit this personnel in accordance with civil service regulations but the management of the federal service extends far beyond the confines of the merit system.

When the Hoover Commission on Organization of the Executive Branch of the Government made its report in 1949, stress was placed upon the need for an Office of Personnel to be established in the President's office in order to provide the President with continuous staff advice and assistance relative to matters affecting the civilian service of the federal government. The director of the Office of Personnel was to be the chairman of the United States Civil Service Commission. Basic changes in the field of personnel administration were also recommended, nearly all of which were designed to improve the career opportunities for employment in the government of the United States.

The Hoover Commission report was in many respects a great improvement upon that of the President's Committee on Administrative Management. It recognized more clearly the problems to be solved, but failed completely to provide adequate solutions. If the report had followed its statement of the problems by adopting the solutions proposed by the minority member of the commission a much better document would have resulted. Where the Hoover Commission failed was not in want of vision to discover the evils to be cured but in lack of courage to press for the right remedies. The report appears to be a compromise at precisely those points where straightforwardness is required.

The majority report recommends that personnel administration be decentralized under "standards approved by the Civil Service Commission." This is about what is being done at present. The United States Civil Service Commission has never been much more than a recruiting agency, and increasingly in the years following World War II the work of recruitment has had to be done by the operating departments and agencies. The time has probably arrived when the operating departments can do a better job of finding and qualifying personnel than the technicians of the Civil Service Commission. Mr. Hoover and his associates would have been more in step with the times if they had advised the complete decentralization of personnel administration, leaving the operating departments free to compete in the development of procedures adapted to their own peculiar needs. The controls of a central personnel agency would be utilized only where departments failed to comply with the law or defaulted in carrying out the tasks assigned to them.

The greatest weakness in the majority report is the compromise which continues the Civil Service Commission but makes the chairman responsible for administration. The effect of this compromise is to reduce the other members of the commission to a status where they can offer little of value to the government. The authority will be in the chairman, he alone will have access to the President and will command the attention and respect of the public employees and public officials. A strong chairman who enjoys the confidence of the President may be neither helped nor hindered by his association with a commission. There can be no sound reason for the continued existence of the Civil Service Commission if the main objectives of the Hoover Commission report are to be achieved. The Civil Service Commission should have been replaced by a single personnel officer who would function as adviser to the President and the department heads on all matters of personnel administration. The merit system is merely one of the statutory constructions, the machinery of which the personnel officer would operate in the interest of securing fewer and better public employees.

The merit system has too long been one of the "sacred cows" among American political institutions. Created to thwart the spoilsman, it has evolved a set of procedural regulations the unraveling of which consumes time and energy and contributes to the waste of public funds. A frontal attack upon the red tape and inefficiency of any civil service system will be met by loud outcries from its beneficiaries and their friends that a return to the spoils system is threatened. This is merely a confusion of the issue to gratify selfish interests. The choice is seldom between the maintenance of the existing civil service system and the indiscriminate distribution of the patronage. All that is desired is more efficient administration of the personnel which has been selected on a basis of merit and fitness. There is nothing sacrosanct about the merit system.

The obeisance of the Hoover Commission to the established institutions of the federal civil service system is all the more surprising because there exist in some of the states better methods of personnel administration. The merit system law in Maryland has long been the most precise statement of the purposes of civil service reform, and the organization through which it operates is today the most successful in the United States.

The Maryland merit system law protects the civil service employee at the same time that it exacts from him the full measure of his ability in the performance of his duties. Its purpose is "to provide candidates for appointment to positions in the classified service after determining by practical tests of the fitness of such candidates for the positions which they seek, without regard to the political or religious opinions or affiliations of such candidates, or of any other standard except the business efficiency of the classified service, and to provide adequate means for the prompt removal from positions in the classified service of all persons therein who may be indolent, incompetent, inefficient, or otherwise unfit to remain therein. . . ." This concise statement embodies the whole of the merit system. It safeguards the equality of opportunity in appointments at the same time that it assures speedy removal from public employment in the event of ascertained unfitness.

The State Employment Commission in Maryland comprises a single commissioner who is directly responsible to the governor by whom he is appointed. The commissioner is not merely the administrator of the merit system but also the personnel officer whose advice and assistance are available to the governor whenever required. In a recent decision the State Employment Commissioner stated his functions as follows: "The merit system was enacted to prevent the removal for political or religious motives of loyal, conscientious, and efficient employees. The present Commissioner is determined to prevent any violation of this principle and as Chief Personnel Officer of the State he is also opposed to nepotism, favoritism, or any other type of unfair treatment of the employees of the State.

"On the other hand, classified employees must recognize that merit system status is not a guarantee of unconditional permanent job tenure. Section 19 of Article 64A provides that no removal shall be allowed because of the religious or political opinions or affiliations of any employee but there is no provision in the law or rules against the removal of any merit system employee for causes which would result in his dismissal from private employment. The best guarantee which any person should rely upon to hold any job is to so perform his duties as to create a desire in his superior to retain him in that job. In these days of rising governmental costs, the taxpayer is entitled to know that the civil servant who does not produce satisfactory work is no more likely to be retained in his job than he would be if he were engaged in private industry." When the merit system is administered in this way it becomes a valuable instrument of public personnel administration and not a defense of assumed vested interests of public personnel.

Judicial review of the acts of administrative officers will be granted freely by the courts where questions of law are involved. In most civil service jurisdictions the courts have held that the dismissal of a public employee is subject to review only as to issues of law involved, except where the statute specifically requires a review of the facts in evidence as well as the law. This is not true in California, Illinois and New Jersey, where the courts have indicated that they will grant a review "in the nature of a trial" on both the facts and the law. Judicial review in these states has not seriously handicapped the administration of the civil service system but it has involved a waste of public money. As long as the courts will continue to grant a generous judicial review of the decisions of administrators and administrative agencies, there will come to burden the judges a procession of contentious folks who think they can put over on the court what they failed to get past the administrator.

Litigation involving civil service matters is undesirable, unless the issues are rigidly confined to questions of law. The constitutional guarantees limit the executive as well as the legislative branches of the government, and arbitrary and capricious administration of the law should be checked by the courts. Law-enforcement with an evil eye and a partial hand may destroy the constitutional guarantees which safeguard the people even more certainly than the enactment of bad legislation. But the issues which public employees seek to bring before the courts ordinarily do not involve contraventions of the law. The administrator, mindful of the political effects of his acts, has nearly always complied with the law. What the litigious employee seeks is a judge who will substitute his judgment for that of the administrator who has already decided against him. It is to the credit of the courts in this country that few judges of this kind can be found.

The urgent present day need is the establishment of personnel offices at all levels of government through which the merit system can be administered in subordination to the chief executive. The merit system should be made an effective device for the recruitment of the best men and women who have been trained in the schools, colleges, and universities of the country and who desire to enter public employment. It must not be perverted into an agency whereby the security of tenure which it provides will continue on public payrolls the incompetent and those whose services are no longer required. When civil service departments have become personnel departments sufficiently flexible to meet the demands of changing circumstances, the costs of government can be reduced at the same time that improved public services are rendered through the employment of better people.

CHAPTER VI

THE UNFINISHED BUSINESS

THIS book has presented an argument for the establishment of greater administrative control of public personnel in the hands of the chief executive. In the accomplishment of this purpose further efforts must be made by civil service reform. Three fundamental reforms are necessary to enable civil service systems to function efficiently in present day governments:

1. The amateur bipartisan civil service commissions should be replaced by personnel departments under the direction of a single commissioner responsible to the chief executive. The time has passed when a civil service department can be maintained external to the administrative hierarchy without sacrificing much that is essential to good government. The merit system is merely a device through which to recruit the best qualified people for public employment. Both the President's Committee on Administrative Management in 1937 and the Hoover Commission on Organization of the Executive Branch of the Government in 1949 diagnosed the ailments which afflict personnel administration at the present time but neither investigation led to a cure. Having introduced the merit system into the federal government and the governments of many states and municipalities, civil service reform must now strive to enable the chief executive to utilize the public personnel to the best advantage to accomplish the purposes of government.

2. There should be created by law adequate machinery to solve the problems of employer-employee relationships. Between public officials and the employees of

government there must be a genuine partnership if the public services are to be efficiently performed. Few genuine grievances arise as a result of violations of civil service laws and regulations. The most common causes of complaints fall wholly outside the provisions of civil service laws and are incapable of inclusion within the normal jurisdiction of civil service departments. Government must provide the means for regular and continuous cooperation between the officers and employees of government to remove the causes of grievances and to promote the solution of problems in the service. Representatives of the public employees must have ready access at all times to the officers of government. Whether the employees are organized in unions or in independent civil service associations not engaged in collective bargaining is a matter for the employees to decide. Where honest differences of opinion arise between department or agency heads and the public employees, negotiations should not be terminated but the dispute should be transferred to some impartial tribunal where the paramount public interest may pronounce a final decision. In other words, there must be set up in the law some competent scheme of arbitration.

3. Citizen organizations interested in the promotion and extension of the merit system should be strengthened. The safeguards of the merit system remain precisely what they were in the early days of civil service reform—an enlightened electorate which recognizes the evils, nuisance, and waste of the spoils system. It is idle to suppose that civil service commissions comprised of political appointees will become staunch defenders of the merit system. The members of such commissions are sometimes busy manipulating the civil service system in the interest of party organizations. The defense of the merit system can be assured only through citizen

groups such as the National Civil Service League. The members of these citizen groups should look beyond the recruitment of public personnel to the efficient management of the civil service. In effect, the ideals of civil service reform are identical with those of economy and efficiency in government.

INDEX